Geographical Names
of the
Ellesmere Island
National Park Reserve
and Vicinity

by

Geoffrey Hattersley-Smith

Parks Canada – Parcs Canada

The Arctic Institute of North America

Published by the Arctic Institute of North America
of the University of Calgary
2500 University Drive N.W.
Calgary, Alberta, Canada T2N 1N4

Canadian Cataloguing in Publication Data

Hattersley-Smith, G., 1923-
   Geographical names of the Ellesmere Island National Park
Reserve and vicinity

   Copublished by: Parks Canada.
   Includes bibliographical references.
   ISBN 0-919034-96-9

   I. Names, Geographical—Northwest Territories—Ellesmere
Island. 2. Ellesmere Island National Park Reserve (N.W.T.)—
History. 3. Ellesmere Island (N.W.T.)—Discovery and
exploration. I. Arctic Institute of North America. II. Parks
Canada. III. Title.
FC4195.E44A33 1998   971.1'5   c98-910148-7
F1105.E44H37 1998

Credits:

Copyediting by Luisa Alexander Izzo
Cartography by Marilyn Croot, Sun Mountain Graphics, Calgary, Alberta
Design and production by Jeremy Drought, Last Impression Publishing, Calgary, Alberta
Printed and bound by Printcrafters Inc., Winnipeg, Manitoba

Cover photos:

Front cover: "*Tanquary Camp with Gull Glacier,*" from the painting
               by Maurice Haycock, B.Sc., Ph.D., D.C.L. (Hon.), 26 July 1965
Back cover: Photograph of Geoffrey Hattersley-Smith by A.G.F. Ditcham

In memory of

Albert Crary
James Croal
Roger Deane
Trevor Harwood
&

Harold Serson

Companions in the field

Contents

Map of Ellesmere Island National Park Reserve and Vicinity (back pocket).

List of Illustrations

1. *Barbeau Peak* (2616 m), the highest mountain in eastern North America, with the *British Empire Range* in the background.

2. *Johns Island,* basking in the 24-hour sunlight.

3. Looking south through the *Rollrock River* valley, one can see *Rollrock Lake,* which is blocked from drainage by *Rollrock Glacier.* Further along and to the left is *Steeprock Glacier,* and in the distance is *Tanquary Fiord.*

4. *Air Force Glacier.*

5. *Gull Glacier* at the head of *Tanquary Fiord.*

6. The *Fort Conger* National Historic Site, located on the northeastern shore of *Discovery Harbour,* seen looking towards *Mount Campbell* on *Bellot Island.*

7. Junction of the *Scylla* (left) and *Charybdis* (right) *Glaciers* as seen from *Mount Biederbick,* located along the *Lewis River* valley. Blocked by giant glaciers on either side sits *Ekblaw Lake.*

8. August breakup of *Lake Hazen* as seen from *McGill Mountain.*

9. Herd of arctic hares in the upper *Snow Goose River* valley.

10. Cairn at *Record Point* in *Archer Fiord.*

11. *Fiala Glacier* at the head of the *Air Force River* valley.

12. Looking northwest through *Bellows Valley.*

13. *Omingmak Mountain* on the north shore of *Lake Hazen.*

14. Looking towards *Discovery Harbour* from the shore of *Heintzelman Lake.*

15. The mountains of the *British Empire Range* pierce through the surrounding permanent icefields, up to 900 m thick and estimated to be more than 100,000 years old.

16. *Walker Hill* on *Ward Hunt Island.* Note the *Ward Hunt Ice Shelf* in the foreground.

Preface

THERE are 382 officially accepted geographical names in the area of northeastern Ellesmere Island treated in this work, which includes the Ellesmere Island National Park Reserve. Since 1897, the Canadian Permanent Committee on Geographical Names (formerly known successively as the Geographic Board of Canada and the Canadian Board on Geographical Names) has had the overall authority for the adoption of names. The background to this Committee and a review of its principles are provided. A review is then given of the evolution of the geographical names as a result of voyages of discovery, scientific and other expeditions, and the field work of departments of the Canadian government. The names are then treated systematically according to prescribed rules, and listed alphabetically. Each entry gives the latitude and longitude of the feature; the locality in relation to neighbouring features; details of discovery, mapping, and naming (in chronological order); and references to first publication of the name (with any synonyms) and to the most recent Canadian government map. Cross-references link more than 100 synonyms to these entries, which include seven Pan-Canadian names officially approved in both English and French. The entries also include five names formerly approved for official use but now obsolete. A number of names that have been published, but not adopted for official use, are not listed.

Acknowledgements

GRATEFUL acknowledgement is made to the following: Dr. Philip Goldring (National Historic Sites Directorate, Parks Canada, Ottawa), for encouragement and advice; Miss Helen Kerfoot (Executive Secretary, Canadian Permanent Committee on Geographical Names, Ottawa), for her time and expertise in guidance through the records of her Committee; Mr. Renee Wissink (former Acting Chief Park Warden, Ellesmere Island National Park Reserve, Pangnirtung), for support, encouragement, and the opportunity to revisit northern Ellesmere Island; Mr. Barry Troke (who succeeded Mr. Wissink), for seeing the work through publication; Mr. Ken Atherton (Hydrographic Office, Ministry of Defence, U.K.), for access to early British Admiralty charts of the Arctic; Mr. P.J.M. Geelan (former Secretary, U.K. Permanent Committee on Geographical Names), for advice; Dr. Karen McCullough (Editor, *Arctic*) for overseeing the production of the book; and to Karole Pittman and the rest of the Haycock family for permission to use one of Maurice Haycock's paintings from the Ellesmere Island National Park Reserve on the cover.

Introduction

THE region of northeastern Ellesmere Island treated in this history of geographical names is that covered by five map sheets in the 1:250,000 series of the Department of Energy, Mines and Resources (DEMR). It includes the whole of the Ellesmere Island National Park Reserve (EINPR), which makes up about two-thirds of the region (EINPR, 1991).

Although the region was known to the Inuit 4,000 years ago and, at least in some periods, was sparsely inhabited year-round, it appears for unknown reasons to have been abandoned as a hunting ground 400–500 years ago and to have been forgotten even in Inuit legend. There is no surviving tradition of Inuit geographical names, and thus no reason to depart from the set of English-language names that has evolved gradually since 1852. Yet it is most fitting that, among the 382 official names listed in this history, four resourceful and renowned Inughuit (Greenlandic) travellers—Egingwah, Nukapinguaq, Ooblooyah and Ootah—should be commemorated.

Authority for the Geographical Names

UNTIL 1897, the source for geographical names in northeastern Ellesmere Island (and elsewhere in the Canadian Arctic) was the British Admiralty (BA), through its production of charts, regularly updated to show the names applied to newly discovered features by successive expeditions (in this case BA chart 275, 1875, and later editions).

In 1897, the Geographic Board of Canada (GBC) was established by order-in-council to regulate the geographical names of the whole country and to formulate principles for the identification and naming of features. For the Arctic the GBC thus took over the function of standardizing names, previously the role of the British Admiralty.

In 1910, the Board published a definitive listing of approved geographical names for northern Canada, including about 90 names in northeastern Ellesmere Island (GBC, 1910). In 1948, the Board was renamed as the Canadian Board on Geographical Names (CBGN). Between 1910 and 1948, only five expeditions ventured briefly into northeastern Ellesmere Island, and fewer than 20 new names were added to the approved list. After 1948, a surge of activity in the region led to the adoption of more than 250 new geographical names. In 1961, the Board was renamed as the Canadian Permanent Committee on Geographical Names (CPCGN), and a representative from the Department of Indian Affairs and Northern Development became responsible for Northwest Territories naming (CPCGN, 1990:IV). Since 1984, the Government of the Northwest Territories in Yellowknife has managed its own

1

Geographical Names Program, passing on its decisions to the CPCGN based in Ottawa, where the Secretariat maintains a complete record of all geographical names in Canada on the Canadian Geographical Names Data Base.

Principles of Geographical Naming

ENERAL principles of geographical naming take into account five main considerations:

1. The purpose of a name is to supply a means of identifying a feature beyond doubt.
2. Permanence in naming can be ensured only by correct identification of features, and by avoidance of duplication or ambiguity in the use of names.
3. The priority of the original names applied to features should be preserved, whenever possible.
4. An existing name, once it has been accepted, should not be altered without very good reason.
5. As a general rule, a name should be rejected if its accurately determined position is found to differ greatly from its earlier reported position(s).

The guiding principles of the Canadian Permanent Committee on Geographical Names add detail to these primary considerations (CPCGN, 1990), and can be readily summarized in their application to naming in northeastern Ellesmere Island.

No name is acceptable unless adequate information on its origin and on the position and nature of the feature is available. Names should be concise, euphonious, and in good taste, avoiding unnatural or incongruous combinations of words, corrupted names, and names of obscure origin. To avoid confusion, especially for features in the same general area, duplication of names should also be avoided, although this has sometimes occurred through oversight.

The main sources of geographical names for northeastern Ellesmere Island have included descriptive adjectives appropriate to the features, and the names of local fauna and flora, explorers of the region and other Arctic explorers, expedition sponsors, prominent persons in the countries of origin of expeditions, and Canadian war dead. In recent years, it has been the general policy of the Committee not to name features after living persons, although exceptions have been made in the case of a few major Arctic features named after members of the Royal Family, Governors General, and outstanding Canadian explorers of the region.

A few names used for features in northeastern Ellesmere Island, detailed on page 16, have been rendered obsolete either through lack of identification, poor definition, or—in the case of an ice shelf—disappearance. At the same time, the official naming of small features of local significance, as near Alert or near field

2

stations, has been constrained by the lack of published maps at large enough scale to show the features.

Since all the geographical names in northeastern Ellesmere Island were originally applied in English, there has been no need to translate or transcribe original names, except for a few Pan-Canadian names and the specific parts of a few Inuit names, detailed on page 17.

Origin of the Geographical Names

IN the 19th century, the evolution of geographical names in northeastern Ellesmere Island followed the progression of exploring ships northward up Smith Sound and beyond, sometimes called "the American route to the North Pole," because these were all American ships, with the notable exception of the British Arctic Expedition (BAE) ships. There was then little activity contributing to new geographical names until after World War II when, with the advent of icebreakers and aircraft in the region, a burst of new naming took place (Hattersley-Smith, 1964a).

The expeditions and agencies that contributed to the geographical names of northeastern Ellesmere Island are summarized below and in Appendix I. Two other expeditions passed along the shores of the region. In the spring of 1920, the Third Thule Expedition, under the leadership of Captain Godfred Hansen of the Royal Danish Navy, laid caches at Fort Conger and Cape Columbia in support of Roald Amundsen's planned North Polar drift in the *Maud*. At the same time, the Danish Bicentenary Expedition to North Greenland, under the leadership of Lauge Koch, spent a few days at Fort Conger on its way around North Greenland. However, neither of these expeditions contributed to the geographical names.

Edward Augustus Inglefield, 1852

In 1852, Commander E.A. (later Admiral Sir Edward) Inglefield, RN, commanded the SY *Isabel* on a Franklin search expedition, which became the first to penetrate as far north as Smith Sound. In late August of that year, he reached his farthest north (78°28′21″N) in that sound. In his account of the expedition (Inglefield, 1853), he was meticulous in recording the origin of the names that he applied to newly discovered features. The only one of these names relevant to the present map area is *Ellesmere Island* for the land on the west coast of northern Baffin Bay, northward from Jones Sound to Smith Sound. Later expeditions were to use the name *Ellesmere Land* for this territory, until the definition of the insularity of Ellesmere Island by Otto Sverdrup (1904).

Elisha Kent Kane, 1853–55

In 1853–55, Dr. E.K. Kane, USN, led a Franklin search expedition in the SY *Advance*, which became known as the Second Grinnell Expedition, after its principal sponsor. The expedition spent the 1853–54 winter at Rensselaer Bugt, at 78°37′N on the Greenland coast. In May–June 1854, a sledge party under the expedition surgeon, Dr. I.I. Hayes, crossed Smith Sound to Cape Sabine, Ellesmere Island, and explored the east coast of that island as far north as 79°45′N. In July of the same year, another sledge party travelled up the Greenland side of the newly discovered and named *Kennedy Channel* as far north as c. 81°00′N, within sight of the entrance of *Lady Franklin Bay* and *Mount Parry*, named by the expedition.

A total of 10 names applied to newly discovered features within the present map area resulted from these two sledge journeys, together with the now obsolete *Grinnell Land* for the unexplored hinterland of the west coast of Kennedy Channel. There is a degree of uncertainty in the later identifications of some of the features named by Kane, since sightings were made at distances up to 200 km. Those commemorated in the names include Queen Victoria and Prince Albert, Arctic explorers of the Royal Navy, and sponsors of the expedition (Kane, 1856).

The expedition was forced to spend a second winter in North Greenland, by which time two men had died from the effects of scurvy and the health of the others was poor. In May 1855, they abandoned the ice-locked ship and retreated by sledge and by boat, finally reaching the safety of Upernavik in August, to be rescued by a Danish ship.

Isaac Israel Hayes, 1860–61

In 1860–61, following his experience with Kane, Dr. I.I. Hayes led an American expedition in the schooner *United States,* with the objective "to complete the survey of the north coasts of Greenland and Grinnell Land, and to make such explorations as I might find practicable in the direction of the North Pole" (Hayes, 1867:1). In September 1860, the ship reached Etah on the Greenland shore of Smith Sound at 78°20′N, where the expedition wintered. In April–May 1861, Hayes sledged with difficulty across Kane Basin and landed at Cape Hawks on the east coast of Ellesmere Island at 79°30′N. He continued north up that coast, passing his farthest north on Kane's expedition. He claimed to have reached 81°35′N off Lady Franklin Bay. However, later explorers found his descriptions of the coastline very inaccurate, and it is probable that he reached no farther north than c. 80°15′N.

As a result of this sledge journey, Hayes applied seven names to newly discovered features within the present map area, commemorating *inter alia* the Danish King and the expedition ship and sponsors (Hayes, 1867).

The ship broke out of winter quarters in mid-July 1861, when the expedition sailed south for the United States.

Charles Francis Hall/Sidney O. Budington, 1871–73

In July 1871, under the auspices of the United States Navy, Captain C.F. Hall sailed in command of the United States North Polar Expedition in the steam tugboat USS *Polaris* for the main purpose of attaining the North Pole via the Smith Sound route. The *Polaris* made rapid progress northwards through Smith Sound, Kane

4

Basin and Kennedy Channel, and into the newly discovered *Hall Basin, Robeson Channel* and *Lincoln Sea* to reach 82°11′N, the farthest north ever reached by any ship at that time. After being stopped by ice, Hall turned south to find winter quarters at Thank God Harbour, North Greenland, off Hall Basin at 81°38′N. Here Hall died of undetermined causes in November 1871, so that command of the expedition devolved upon the Ice Master Sidney O. Budington.

A total of 19 new geographical names within the present map area have been traced to this expedition, relating mainly to features on the north coast of Ellesmere Island, which were plotted from the ship's northernmost position and identified with reasonable certainty by the British Arctic Expedition that followed four years later. These names commemorate, among others, President Lincoln; senior officers of the U.S. Navy, Army, and civil administration; U.S. scientists; and an Arctic explorer of the Royal Navy, with one descriptive name. The expedition also commemorated another U.S. president in the now obsolete name *Grant Land* for the unexplored hinterland west of Robeson Channel (Davis, 1876).

Following the death of Hall, the *Polaris* remained trapped by ice at Thank God Harbour until mid-August 1872 before the retreat south, which stands as one of the sagas of the sea. The *Polaris* drifted south, but by mid-October it was nipped in the ice of Smith Sound and in danger of foundering. It was decided to abandon ship, and 19 members of the party had been evacuated to an ice floe, when the ship broke free with 14 members of the party still aboard. Contact between ship and ice floe was lost. After a long southerly drift, those on the floe were eventually picked up off the Labrador coast in April 1873. Meanwhile, the ship had managed to reach Etah in North Greenland and, after the winter, the 14 men had set off southward in boats. They were picked up by a Scottish whaler in Melville Bay in June 1873.

George Strong Nares, 1875–76

The British Arctic Expedition, 1875–76, was sent out by the Admiralty for the main purpose of reaching the North Pole via Smith Sound. It was also to explore the adjacent coasts from winter quarters. Captain G.S. (later Vice Admiral Sir George) Nares, RN, commanded the expedition in HMS *Alert*, with HMS *Discovery* in company, commanded by Captain H.F. (later Admiral Sir Henry) Stephenson, RN. Leaving England at the end of May 1875, the two ships made good passage through Smith Sound, Kane Basin, and Kennedy Channel, reaching *Discovery Harbour* in Lady Franklin Bay at the end of August. Here the *Discovery* took up winter quarters, while the *Alert* continued north up Robeson Channel to find winter quarters at *Floeberg Beach*, near Cape Sheridan at 82°28′N, the highest latitude reached by any ship to that time. Fine seamanship marked this feat of navigation, sadly unmatched by the cumbersome equipment and unsuitable clothing of the sledge parties deployed from the two ships over the next 11 months. Dogs had been embarked in West Greenland, but were used unsuccessfully because of poor handling and inadequate feeding. Thus hand sledges were used on the main journeys.

After depot-laying journeys in the fall of 1875, Nares and Stephenson sent out exploring parties in the spring of 1876. The first of these under Sub-Lieutenant G. le C. Egerton, RN, in late March–early April, sledged from the *Alert* to the *Discovery* and back, following the western shore of Robeson Channel. Meanwhile, in early April, a party from the *Alert* under Commander A.H. Markham sledged to Cape Joseph Henry and thence northward over the pack ice to 83°20′N, the farthest north ever reached to that time, before turning back to the ship, which they regained in mid-June. At the same time, another party from the *Alert*, under Lieutenant P. Aldrich, RN, set out to explore and chart the north coast of Ellesmere Island. On this journey, Aldrich established *Cape Columbia* as the northernmost point of land, and then continued west and southwest to Alert Point, on the west side of Yelverton Inlet and well outside the present map area, before turning back to the ship, which he regained in late June. As a measure of the relative accuracy of Aldrich's charting of the coast, it may be noted that his coordinates for Cape Columbia were 83°07′N, 70°30′W as compared with 83°07′N, 69°57′W from the most recent determination. From the *Discovery*, while one party explored the northwestern coast of Greenland, another party under Lieutenant R.H. Archer, RN, in April–May, explored and charted *Archer Fiord* to its head.

All these sledge parties were beset by scurvy, from which four men died. Nares was thus forced to abandon plans for a second year in the Arctic, and his two ships sailed for England in late August 1876. Despite its curtailment and failure to reach the North Pole, the expedition returned with a rich harvest of geographical discoveries and scientific observations and collections (BPP, 1877; Nares, 1878; Hattersley-Smith, 1976).

A total of 105 geographical names within the present area originated on this expedition, and were incorporated on its charts, in published narratives, and on subsequent Admiralty charts. People commemorated in the names number 59, and include one Saint (*Saint Patrick Bay*), Royal personages (e.g., *Cape Albert Edward*), two British prime ministers (*Mount Disraeli, Mount Gladstone*) and other politicians (e.g., *Ward Hunt Island*), contemporary British admirals (e.g., *Mount Hornby*), Arctic explorers (e.g., *Parry Peninsula*), distinguished Americans (e.g., *Mount Grant*), and officers and ratings of the two BAE ships (e.g., *Cape Nares, Dodge Bay*). Exploring ships occur in four names (e.g., *Cape Hecla*) and places elsewhere in four names (e.g., *Winchester Hills*). Of the remaining names, five are after local fauna (e.g., *Oopik Island*), and thirty-three names are either descriptive (e.g., *Rambow Hill*) or connected with incidents on the expedition (e.g., *Depot Point*). The derivation of a few of the personal names has not been established.

Adolphus Washington Greely, 1881–84

The United States Expedition to Lady Franklin Bay was organized by the U.S. Army Signal Service to contribute to the scientific work of the International Polar Year, 1882–83. The 26-man expedition, composed of U.S. Army personnel and two Greenland hunters, was commanded by Lieutenant (later Major General) A.W. Greely. After a good passage through Smith Sound and Kane Basin in August 1881, the expedition landed at Discovery Harbour, Lady Franklin Bay, where HMS *Discovery* had wintered in 1875–76. Here they built their station, named *Fort Conger* after the U.S. Senator E.H. Conger, a supporter of the expedition, and started the prescribed meteorological, magnetic, and tidal observations, which were continued without break for two years.

In the early spring of 1882, while one party set out by dog team and hand sledge to explore the northwestern coast of Greenland, another dog team party under the surgeon, Dr. O. Pavy, travelled north up Robeson Channel and reached a point on the pack ice a short distance north of Cape Joseph Henry, before returning to Fort Conger in early May. Meanwhile, in late April, a party under Greely travelled inland with hand sledges via *Chandler Fiord* and *Ruggles River* to *Lake Hazen*, the principal discovery of the expedition within the EINPR, named by Greely after Major General W.B. Hazen, Chief Signal Officer of the U.S. Army. Greely returned to Fort Conger in early May, but in June–July resumed his exploration of Lake Hazen. On foot and with some use of a hand cart, he travelled to the southwest end of Lake Hazen and beyond up the valley of *Very River* to *Mount Arthur*, which he climbed and named after the then president of the United States. From this point he returned to Fort Conger.

In the spring of 1883, a party under Lieutenant J.B. Lockwood, with both dog sledge and hand sledge, headed up Archer Fiord to cross Ellesmere Island via the valley of *Dodge River* and, skirting *Agassiz Ice Cap*, reached the sea ice at the head of *Greely Fiord*. They returned to Fort Conger by the same route at the end of May.

Since the relief ship had failed to reach Fort Conger during two summers, Greely decided in August 1883 to retreat south in the expedition launch with three small boats in tow. He and his party were forced to winter near Cape Sabine, eastern Ellesmere Island on Smith Sound, where, living in a stone hut, they faced starvation. When the relief ship arrived in late June 1884, only Greely and six others remained alive, and one of those men died during the return voyage to the United States. Thus the expedition ended in a disaster with few parallels in the history of Arctic exploration (Greely, 1886, 1888).

A total of 37 official geographical names within the present map area were first applied by Greely, mainly to features around the shores of Lake Hazen. Those commemorated included two U.S. presidents and a senator, senior U.S. Navy and Army officers, American scientists and Arctic navigators, relatives of Greely, and members of the Lady Franklin Bay Expedition (LFBE). The derivation of a number of the names has not been established.

Robert Edwin Peary, 1898–1902, 1905–06, 1908–09

R.E. Peary, USN, privately organized and led three expeditions to northern Ellesmere Island in 1898–1902, 1905–06, and 1908–09. (In 1898 he was a Lieutenant, but he had risen to Commander by 1905 and retired from the navy in 1911 as a Rear Admiral.) For all his expeditions he employed Inughuit guides from the Thule District, North Greenland. He developed a system of travel by dog sledge of unsurpassed efficiency.

In 1898, in his ship SY *Windward*, Peary wintered at Cape d'Urville, eastern Ellesmere Island, off Kane Basin. During the winter he sledged north to Fort Conger, where he dismantled Greely's house to construct three small huts (Hattersley-Smith, 1964b; Dick, 1991). During his return journey to the ship in February 1899, he lost most of his toes through frostbite; but two months later, he went back to Fort Conger for an unsuccessful attempt to cross Robeson Channel to the Greenland coast. At the end of May, he was back in his ship, which later took him across to Etah, North Greenland, where he wintered. In March 1900, Peary sledged north again to Fort Conger and then explored for the first time the whole northern coast of Greenland, before returning to Fort Conger for the winter. Meanwhile, the *Windward*, on a relief voyage, reached Payer Harbour, eastern Ellesmere Island, on Smith Sound, where she was forced to winter. In May 1901, Peary rejoined his ship at Payer Harbour, wintering there while the ship returned south. In March 1902, he set out for his first attempt on the North Pole. Travelling north via Fort Conger, he reached 84°17′N, north of Cape Hecla, his farthest north yet. He then returned to Payer Harbour, where he was picked up by the *Windward* for return to the United States (Peary, 1907).

On his expedition of 1905–06 in the ss *Roosevelt*, with the Newfoundlander Captain R.A. Bartlett as Ice Master, Peary wintered his ship at Cape Sheridan, near where Nares had wintered in 1875–76. In early spring 1906, he made his second unsuccessful attempt to reach the North Pole, leaving the land at Cape Hecla and reaching the record latitude of 87°06′N, before being forced back on the Greenland coast. Within a week of his return to the ship, he set out in early June with the Inughuit guides Egingwah and Ooblooyah to explore the northwest coast of Ellesmere Island between Aldrich's farthest west at Alert Point (BPP, 1877:212; Nares, 1878, Vol. 2:29) and Sverdrup's farthest north at Lands Lokk on Nansen Sound (Sverdrup, 1904, Vol. I:358). He returned to the ship at the end of July, having achieved his objective and having crossed Nansen Sound to Cape Stallworthy, the northernmost point of Axel Heiberg Island. From a vantage point on that journey, he claimed to have sighted new land far to the northwest, which he called "Crocker Land." What he saw was probably a mirage, or possibly an ice island. After severe damage in Robeson Channel, the *Roosevelt* returned safely to the United States in late November 1906 (Peary, 1907).

On his last expedition of 1908–09, again with Captain Bartlett in the *Roosevelt*, Peary wintered at Cape Sheridan as before. At the end of February 1909, he left for the North Pole with supporting parties under Bartlett, G. Borup, J.W. Godsell, R.G. Marvin, and D.B. MacMillan. He claimed to have reached the North Pole on 6 April, with his party comprising his black assistant Matthew Henson and the Inughuit guides Egingwah, Ookeah, Ootah, and Seegloo. Whether or not he reached the North Pole will remain in controversy, although it is most probable that he reached within a radius of, say, 10–20 km of that elusive point on floating ice (Hattersley-Smith, 1961b). By the end of April, Peary had returned to the *Roosevelt*, which sailed for home in mid-July (Peary, 1910).

Peary is remembered as one of the most undaunted travellers in history. Yet any interest he may have had in the region he travelled was completely overshadowed by his desire to reach the North Pole and to discover new land, as in 1900 and 1906. He showed little concern for the explorations of his predecessors, as strikingly demonstrated by his failure to recover three records in cairns on the north coast of Ellesmere Island, left by the British Arctic Expedition in 1876. He applied names to four features on the newly discovered coast southwest of Alert Point, and well outside the present map area, but within this area only one official geographical name has been traced to his expeditions: *Sheridan River*, named in association with Cape Sheridan.

Donald Baxter MacMillan, 1913–17

The United States Crocker Land Expedition, 1913–17, was privately organized and led by D.B. MacMillan (later Rear Admiral, U.S. Naval Reserve), who had previously served under Peary in 1908–09. The expedition was based at Etah, North Greenland, where four winters were spent, and its main purpose was to search for Peary's mythical "Crocker Land," supposed to lie in the Arctic Ocean to the north of Axel Heiberg Island. A long sledge journey to that region by a party under MacMillan in the spring of 1914 virtually dispelled any belief in the existence of "Crocker Land" (MacMillan, 1918).

In the spring of 1915, the expedition made its only incursion into the present map area. The expedition geologist and botanist W.E. Ekblaw, with the Inughuit guides Etookashoo and Esayoo, crossed Smith Sound to Flagler Bay and then crossed Ellesmere Island to Bay Fiord, continuing north up Eureka Sound to Greely Fiord. Between late April and mid-May, Ekblaw discovered and named *Borup Fiord* (outside the present map area) and *Tanquary Fiord*, which he explored and roughly mapped throughout their length. In the environs of Tanquary Fiord, and within the present area, he applied a total of 19 new geographical names, later adopted for official use. The fiord itself was named after M.C. Tanquary, the zoologist on the expedition, and other names commemorated Arctic explorers, American and Canadian biologists and geologists (including staff of the American Museum of Natural History), university administrators, an American congressman, and a banker, some of whom had been particularly supportive of the expedition.

On the return journey, Ekblaw explored Greely Fiord to its head and then, after negotiating a steep ravine to the plateau, crossed Ellesmere Island via Lake Hazen and Ruggles River to Chandler Fiord and Lady Franklin Bay. He then travelled via Kennedy Channel and Kane Basin back to Etah, which he reached in mid-June (Ekblaw *in* MacMillan, 1918).

Further explorations in the Queen Elizabeth Islands, but outside the present map area, occupied the expedition in the following two seasons, before the return home by relief ship in August 1917.

Gordon Noel Humphreys, 1934–35

The Oxford University Ellesmere Land Expedition (OUELE), 1934–35, was led by Dr. G.N. Humphreys and organized by Edward Shackleton (later Baron Shackleton of Burley). Based at Etah, North Greenland, the six-man expedition, assisted by Inughuit guides, made three main sledge journeys in the spring of 1935, of which only the northern journey is relevant to the present map area.

In April, Sergeant H.W. Stallworthy, RCMP, A.W. Moore, and the Inughuit guides Inutuk and Nukapinguaq sledged north to Lake Hazen. Here Stallworthy and Inutuk established a fishing camp on the lake, while Moore and Nukapinguaq continued up Gilman Glacier to *Mount Oxford*, of which they made the first known ascent. Moore overestimated its height as 9,000 ft (2750 m), and the height of the *British Empire Range* observed to the north as more than 10,000 ft (3050 m) (Shackleton, 1937; Hattersley-Smith, 1958). The four-man party returned to Etah at the end of May. The above two names were the only new geographical names applied by the expedition within the present map area, although these were not adopted for official use until 1960. The expedition returned safely to England in late September 1935.

James van Hauen, 1939–40

The Danish Thule and Ellesmere Land Expedition, 1939–40, was privately organized and comprised five Danes under the leadership of J. van Hauen. The expedition was based at Neqe, North Greenland, and was assisted by Inughuit guides.

In April–May 1940, two parties crossed Ellesmere Island via Flagler Bay and Bay Fiord to explore western Ellesmere Island and Axel Heiberg Island. The northernmost of the two parties comprised van Hauen, J.C. Troelsen, M. Rasmussen, and the Inughuit guides Baadsmand, Magassanguaq, and Qarkutsiaq, with his wife Padloq. They travelled north up Eureka and Nansen Sounds, and returned via Otto and Hare Fiords to the head of Greely Fiord, where they discovered the glacier-dammed *Lake Tuborg*—the only new geographical name applied by the expedition within the present map area, which was not adopted for official use until 1965. From Lake Tuborg, the party crossed overland to Hall Basin via Nan Lake, Dodge River, and Archer Fiord, and returned to Neqe via Kennedy Channel and Kane Basin (Vibe, 1948; Hattersley-Smith, 1968).

The five Danes of the expedition returned south in September 1940, but did not see their homeland again until the end of the war.

Royal Canadian Air Force, 1946–60

In 1946–47, the United States Air Force carried out a series of long-range reconnaissance flights over the Queen Elizabeth Islands and the Arctic Ocean in specially equipped B-29 aircraft, departing from Edmonton, Alberta, and Fairbanks, Alaska. Air crews included several members of the Royal Canadian Air Force (RCAF). The first extensive air photographic coverage of northern Ellesmere Island resulted from these flights (Greenaway and Colthorpe, 1948:53–102). In 1950, as part of the mapping programme for northern Canada, the RCAF flew flight lines for trimetrogon photography covering the whole of northern Ellesmere Island, using World War II Lancaster aircraft with a camera mounted in the bomb bay (Dunbar and Greenaway, 1957:249–337). The resultant maps, published in the Department of Mines and Technical Services (DMTS) 1:500,000 series, were a vast improvement on the maps and charts produced by explorers, mainly of the 19th century.

In 1959–60, the RCAF flew flight lines for vertical air photography over the whole of northern Ellesmere Island, and in 1962 an airborne field party under P.C. Atkinson, of the Topographical Survey Division, DMTS, established ground control for the region by tellurometric triangulation. The further improved maps were published in the Department of Energy, Mines and Resources (DEMR) 1:250,000 series. Thus, although the RCAF did not itself propose new geographical names, its work enabled proper identification and description of many features for which field scientists needed names.

Canadian Meteorological Service, 1950

In August 1950, the Canadian Meteorological Service, in conjunction with the United States Weather Bureau, established the Joint Arctic Weather Station *Alert*, named after HMS *Alert* of the British Arctic Expedition. Sealift was provided by an icebreaker task force of the United States Navy and Coast Guard. Apart from its main purpose, the station provided a base from which field parties were deployed in subsequent years.

Canadian Geographical Branch, 1952, 1958

In the summer of 1952, P. Gadbois and C. Laverdière were based at the weather station Alert for two months, during which they carried out a geomorphological reconnaissance of the surrounding area. Their work resulted in the adoption of 31 new geographical names. A number of features were named descriptively or in association with features already named. Other names commemorated officers and ratings of HMS *Alert* (e.g., *Egerton Lake, Hollins Creek*), two Canadian officers killed in World War II (*Bowery Inlet, Smith Peninsula*), and a Canadian geographer killed in an air crash at Alert (*Kirk Creek, Kirk Lake*). Further new names in this area resulted from the work of Geographical Branch officers in the summer of 1958.

Canadian Defence Research Board (and associated agencies), 1953–72

The Defence Research Board's interest in northern Ellesmere Island was focused in 1953–54 on the ice shelves of the north coast. The Board was then charged with organizing a scientific operation in the Arctic as part of Canada's contribution to the circumpolar programme of the International Geophysical Year, 1957–58. The Lake Hazen area was chosen for the field research on the advice of T.A. Harwood. In 1963, the Board transferred its main operation to Tanquary Fiord, primarily in order to carry out oceanographic research in the waters of the Nansen Sound fiord system (Hattersley-Smith et al., 1955; Hattersley-Smith, 1956, 1961a, 1964a, 1974; Ford and Hattersley-Smith, 1965).

From Alert, 1953: By 1953, it had become clear that ice shelves off the north coasts of Ellesmere Island were the principal, if not the only, source of the floating ice islands of the Arctic Ocean, of which T-3 became the best known as a drifting station for scientific observations in the Arctic Ocean (Koenig et al., 1952). In that season the Defence Research Board joined with the Geological Survey of Canada, with support from the United States Air Force, in fielding a small party based at Alert from late April to mid-August. G. Hattersley-Smith, of the Defence Research Board (DRB), and R.G. Blackadar, of the Geological Survey of Canada (GSC), were assisted by the Inughuit guides Rasmus Majak and Sigssuk, from the Thule District, North Greenland. Travelling by dog sledge from Alert as far west as Markham Fiord in the spring, they made a reconnaissance of the ice shelves and geology of the coast. During the summer, travelling on foot from Alert, they made a geological reconnaissance southwestward and westward to the head of Wood River, to Mount Grant (which they climbed), *Eugene Glacier, James Ross River,* and Clements Markham Inlet; and also eastward and southeastward to the Sheridan River. Their work resulted in the adoption of four new geographical names, all associated with previously named features.

From Ward Hunt Ice Shelf, 1954: In the 1954 season, a four-man Canadian-United States party under the leadership of G. Hattersley-Smith, of the DRB, was airlifted to Ward Hunt Ice Shelf by ski-wheel C-47 aircraft of the United States Air Force (USAF) North East Air Command from Thule Air Base, North Greenland. The other members of the party were A.P. Crary of the U.S. Air Force Cambridge Research Center (AFCRC), R.L. Christie of the GSC, and E.W. Marshall of the United States Army Cold Regions Research and Engineering Laboratory (CRREL). They were assisted for the first two months by the veteran Inughuit travellers Imina and Qarkutsiaq from the Thule District, with two dog teams, one of which they left behind for the rest of the season.

The party established a base camp on the ice shelf west of Ward Hunt Island, from where they made detailed investigations of the topography, structure, and temperature regime of the ice shelf. They also made a geological and ice reconnaissance by dog sledge of the coast between Cape Columbia and Lands Lokk, Nansen Sound. The party was evacuated by air to Thule Air Base at the end of September.

The field work resulted in the adoption of five new geographical names within the present main area. *Borup Point* and *Marvin Islands* were named after members of Peary's North Pole expedition, 1908–09, and the other three names were associated with previously named features.

From Hazen Camp, 1957–68: The International Geophysical Year Operation Hazen was organized and directed in the field by Dr. G. Hattersley-Smith. The other members of the eight-man party in the 1957 summer comprised Dr. R.L. Christie, and staff and students of McGill University and the University of Toronto. The camp was manned during the winter by four research students of McGill

12

University, led by C.R. Harington. In the 1958 summer, a 19-man party was in the field; included were members of the previous summer party and of the winter party, as well as representatives of the Canadian Fisheries Research Board, Geographical Branch, National Museum (Human History Branch and Natural History Branch), and Wildlife Service.

Hazen Camp was established in late April 1957, following an RCAF airlift involving 10 landings by C-119 aircraft. The first two landings were made on an unprepared airstrip on lake ice with a loose snow cover, previously checked on a landing by a DC-3 ski-wheel aircraft. A bulldozer carried to the site on the first C-119 flight was used to clear a 1000 m airstrip for later landings. In mid-August 1957, the camp was relieved by an icebreaker, the U.S. Coast Guard cutter *Eastwind*, which anchored in Chandler Fiord and deployed helicopters for the changeover of camp personnel and to bring in stores. A similar operation for the evacuation of personnel was carried out by the icebreaker USS *Atka* in mid-August 1958. The operations were coordinated by Lieutenant Commander J.P. Croal, RCN.

In the 1957 and 1958 summers, while six-man parties under Hattersley-Smith operated from a camp on Gilman Glacier, Dr. R.E. Deane of the University of Toronto was in charge of Hazen Camp. Deane and Christie were alone there in 1957, but had a party of 13 in 1958. On foot, and with the help of a small tractor on the ice of Lake Hazen, they made wide-ranging traverses around the shores of the lake, and northeastward, southeastward, and southwestward to Alert, Conybeare Fiord, and the Lewis River. Studies were made in the fields of archaeology, botany, geology, limnology, mammalogy, and ornithology.

From 1962 to 1968, Hazen Camp was reoccupied in the summers for a programme of detailed entomological studies, sponsored by the Canadian Entomology Institute, Department of Agriculture, and coordinated by Dr. D.R. Oliver of that Institute (Oliver, 1963).

As a result of all this field research, a total of 53 new geographical names were adopted for official use. There were two names after members of the Lady Franklin Bay Expedition (*Salor Creek, Whisler Island*), a name after a member of the Crocker Land Expedition (*Ekblaw Lake*), five names associated with agencies participating in the operation (e.g., *Atka Lake, Roundel Glacier, Varsity Mountain*), and seven names after local flora and fauna (e.g., *Dryas Glacier, Weasel Lake*). Mythology was represented in three names (e.g., *Charybdis Glacier*), and places elsewhere in three names (e.g., *Niagara Glacier*). A total of 23 features were named descriptively or in connection with incidents in the field (e.g., *Cuesta Creek, Piper Pass*), and nine features were named in association with previously named features (e.g., *Abbé River*).

From Gilman Glacier Camp, 1957–61, 1967: The six-man parties at the Gilman Glacier camp in the 1957–58 summers, and smaller parties in the 1959–61 and 1967 summers, were engaged in glaciological research and survey work. Dog sledges—and from 1958 on, motor toboggans—were used to travel widely over the central ice cap of northern Ellesmere Island and the upper reaches of the main outlet glaciers. As a result of the work, a total of 15 features were officially named for the first time. Most notable among the new geographical names were *Barbeau Peak* (identified as the highest peak in the Canadian Arctic), after the distinguished Canadian anthropologist Dr. Marius Barbeau; *Commonwealth Mountain*, identified as the highest peak in the British Empire Range; *Air Force Glacier* at the head of Tanquary Fiord, after the RCAF; and *Mount Nukap*, after the veteran Inughuit traveller Nukapinguaq, of the Thule District and of the Oxford University Ellesmere Land Expedition. A further eight features were named descriptively (e.g., *Arrowhead Mountain*), and three features were named in association with features previously named (e.g., *Disraeli Glacier*).

From Tanquary Camp, 1963–72: Following a ground reconnaissance of the upper part of Tanquary Fiord in late May 1962, the site for Tanquary Camp was chosen and, in late August of that year, the icebreaker CCGS *John A. Macdonald* reached the head of the fiord to lay down equipment and stores for the camp. The new Operation Tanquary was organized and directed in the field by Dr. G. Hattersley-Smith; H. Serson of the Defense Research Board supervised the establishment of the camp during the early spring of 1963, and remained a mainstay of the operation in succeeding seasons. Initially, ski-wheel DC-3 aircraft of the RCAF landed on the sea ice with field personnel in the spring. In later seasons, ski-wheel or big-wheel light aircraft were deployed to the nearby airstrip on delta deposits, graded to a length of 1200 m. Except in the severe sea-ice seasons of 1963 and 1964, the camp was resupplied and personnel were evacuated by icebreaker in late August each year.

Each season, an average of 20 field scientists and assistants spent individual periods of a few weeks to five months working from Tanquary Camp. They were drawn from the Canadian Army Survey, Inland Waters Branch, Meteorological Branch, National Museum (Human History Branch), and Topographical Survey; from staff and students of six Canadian universities (Alberta, British Columbia, McGill, New Brunswick, Ottawa, Simon Fraser); and from staff of Cambridge University (U.K.), Dartmouth College (U.S.) and the Smithsonian Institution (U.S.). Research was carried out in the fields of geology, glaciology (including the first airborne radio-echo sounding), limnology, oceanography, and sea-ice physics, and in the fields of archaeology, botany, and marine biology. Routine meteorological observations were maintained in most seasons. Special mention may be made of the work of Count Eigil Knuth, a Danish archaeologist working for the Canadian National Museum in 1966. He confirmed the pre-Dorset age of the ruins near Tanquary Camp discovered in 1962, and thus established the Inuit occupancy of this far northern land 4,000 years ago.

By dog sledge and motor toboggan, with light aircraft support, oceanographic traverses were made of all the fiords of the Nansen Sound system; glaciological work was continued on the central ice cap and on Ward Hunt Ice Shelf and initiated on the ice cap northwest of Tanquary Fiord; and a survey was made of Otto Glacier. Traverses on foot during the summer extended northeast to Ekblaw Lake and Lake

Hazen, southwest to Lake Tuborg, and northwest to Yelverton Pass. A light tractor around the shores and on the sea ice of Tanquary Fiord, and a canoe after ice break-up, assisted the field work.

As a result of the field work, a total of 24 new geographical names were adopted for official use. A Governor General of Canada was commemorated in *Mount Vanier*; the support for the operation by the RCAF was recognized in *Per Ardua Glacier* and *Ad Astra Ice Cap*, and that by the Canadian Coast Guard by *Macdonald River*. Three features were named after local fauna and flora (*Gull Glacier, Silene Creek, Mount Timmia*), and thirteen were named descriptively (e.g., *Green Valley, Rollrock River*), while the remaining four features were named in association with previously named features (e.g., *Yelverton Pass*).

Arctic Institute of North America, 1959–60

In 1959, with the support of the U.S. Air Force Cambridge Research Center, the Arctic Institute of North America (AINA) established a station on Ward Hunt Island, where for two seasons small parties made studies of the ice shelf surrounding the island. In later seasons, the station was used by Defence Research Board field parties. Following the AINA field work, the name *Walker Hill*, after a glaciologist who had taken fatally ill at the station, was officially adopted for the highest feature on the island.

Canadian Department of National Defence, 1962

In 1962, the Department of National Defence established a military station at Alert, later named *Canadian Forces Station Alert*.

Geological Survey of Canada, 1965, 1979, 1980

Following field work by the Geological Survey of Canada from camps established by air on the north coast of Ellesmere Island in 1965, 1979, and 1980, a total of 20 geographical names for features between Ayles Fiord and Disraeli Fiord were adopted for official use. The new names commemorated nine members of the British Arctic Expedition (e.g., *Cranstone Peninsula*), while seven names were after members of Peary's expeditions, including the Inughuit guides Egingwah, Ooblooya, and Ootah. The remaining four names were descriptive (e.g., *Taconite Inlet*).

Canadian Polar Continental Shelf Project, 1972, 1975, 1977

The Polar Continental Shelf Project sponsored geomorphological field work in the Lady Franklin Bay and Archer Fiord area. Following this work, five new geographical names were adopted. One of these names commemorated F.T. Christiansen, a Greenlander with the Lady Franklin Bay Expedition, while the other features were named through association with previously named features, or with local fauna (e.g., *Jaeger Creek*).

15

Royal Naval Ellesmere Island Expedition, 1972

In 1972, the Royal Naval Ellesmere Island Expedition, led by Commander A.B. Erskine, RN, and staged through Tanquary Camp, established by light ski-aircraft a field camp near the head of Milne Glacier. This was primarily a mountaineering expedition, which made first ascents of a number of peaks in the area. Following the expedition, descriptive or allusive names, associated with the Royal Navy and Royal Marines, were adopted for four features (e.g., *Commando Peak*).

Canadian Department of Indian Affairs & Northern Development, 1975

In 1975, at the request of the Department of Indian Affairs and Northern Development, the late Hon. Arthur Laing, of the Canadian Senate, was commemorated in *Arthur Laing Peninsula* on the north coast of Ellesmere Island.

Treatment of the Geographical Names

Systematic Listing

This work provides an alphabetical listing of all the official geographical names (to the end of 1994) in northeastern Ellesmere Island covered by five map sheets in the DEMR 1:250,000 Series. It also includes a few obsolete names, formerly current on maps and charts, and a number of synonyms or variant forms of the official names. Limitations of time and space have not allowed the combing of all relevant publications for unofficial names, and for synonyms or variant forms other than those listed. The treatment of the names follows that used in two previous works, which dealt with Antarctic place-names (Hattersley-Smith, 1980, 1991).

The relevant maps in the DEMR 1:250,000 series are: 120 C & 120 D, Lady Franklin Bay; 120 E, Robeson Channel; 120 F & 120 G, Clements Markham Inlet; 340 D, Tanquary Fiord; and 340 E & 340 H, M'Clintock Inlet.

Categories of Names

Three categories of geographical names are recognized in the alphabetically arranged main entries and cross-references:

- *Approved names.* There are 382 officially approved names listed in upper case.
- *Obsolete names.* These names, listed in lower case, comprise the following: Mount Frere, Grant Land, Grinnell Land, M'Clintock Ice Shelf, and Mount Rawlinson.
- *Synonyms.* These names include variant forms, misnamings and misspellings. The 105 such names listed are shown in italics and cross-referenced to the appropriate approved or obsolete name.

Main Entries

Entries follow the same form for both approved and obsolete names, and include the following information as available and applicable, the arrangement throughout each entry being strictly chronological:

1. Latitude and longitude to the nearest minute (for extended features, with reference to a median point).
2. Locality in relation to neighbouring features and, for a hill or mountain, the height in metres as best determined from the latest map.
3. Details of discovery, first mapping or rough positioning, and naming, together with the reason for the name (if descriptive or allusive) or the person commemorated (if known), including brief biographical data. First namings are italicized.
4. References to first publication of the name, to official approval in original or altered form, and (where applicable) to progressively improved delineation of the feature on maps or charts.
5. References to first publication of synonyms (if any), giving (where appropriate) their origins.

Pan-Canadian Names

Since 1983, certain geographical names have been recognized as Pan-Canadian, of country-wide importance or interest, to be shown on federal government maps in both English and French (CPCGN Decisions, 1983). Such names within the map area of northeastern Ellesmere Island are as follows (in the English form): Canadian Forces Station Alert, Arctic Ocean, Ellesmere Island, Ellesmere Island National Park Reserve, Lincoln Sea, Nares Strait, and Robeson Channel. In the alphabetical listing, the French forms of these names (in upper case) are cross-referenced to the main entries under the English forms.

Inuit Names

The names of the four Inughuit (Greenlandic) travellers, commemorated in the geographical names, together with two Inuit faunal names (Mount Omingmak, Oopik Island), are transcribed according to widely accepted specialist opinion.

Generic Terms

The generic terms used to designate geographical features in the Northwest Territories have been fully listed (CPCGN, 1987). However, in the present context, comment is needed on a few of these terms.

- *Bay, Fiord, Inlet.* A number of major indentations of the north coast of Ellesmere Island were called either *bays* or *inlets* by the early explorers, before their exact nature and extent were known. Several of the *bays* have since been renamed as *fiords* (e.g., Markham Fiord), but the term

17

inlet has been retained in some cases (e.g., Clements Markham Inlet). On the east coast of the island, the term *bay* has been retained for the outer part of the major feature Lady Franklin Bay, while its inner arms are termed *fiords* (e.g., Archer Fiord).

- *Creek.* This term means a small stream—not, as in British usage, a small bay or coastal inlet.
- *Ice Cap.* As used in northeastern Ellesmere Island, the term refers to an extensive area of glacier, with ice-covered peaks and broken by nunataks, rather than to a dome-shaped glacier.
- *Ice Shelf.* Ice shelves are transitory features, as shown by the complete break-up of M'Clintock Ice Shelf (now an obsolete name) and the partial break-up of Ward Hunt Ice Shelf.
- *Lake.* In the earlier naming, this term was usually placed *before* the specific part of a name commemorating a person (e.g., Lake Kilbourne). Later practice has favoured placing the generic part of the name second (e.g., Kilbourne Lake), which avoids the need to reverse word order in alphabetical listing. A number of lake names were thus altered, but not Lake Hazen.
- *Land.* The term was formerly used for an unexplored hinterland (e.g., Ellesmere Land), but is now obsolete.
- *Mount, Mountain, Peak.* Later naming practice has favoured the terms *mountain* and *peak*, rather than *mount*; the use of the latter term forces the reversal of word order in alphabetical listing (cf. *lake*).

Duplication of Names

The name May Creek is regrettably duplicated in a feature near Alert and a feature near Tanquary Camp, although the one is named after a person and the other descriptively.

Alphabetical Order

The alphabetical order follows the letter-by-letter arrangement of the whole name irrespective of word division and irrespective of the comma arising from an inverted generic term. The prefixes *M'* and *Mc* are treated as Mac, and *St.* as Saint.

List of Abbreviations

Abbreviations have been used for agencies, expeditions, and reference sources:

AFCRC	United States. Air Force Cambridge Research Center
AINA	Arctic Institute of North America
BA	Great Britain. Admiralty. Hydrographic Department
BAE	Great Britain. Admiralty. British Arctic Expedition, 1875–76
BPP	Great Britain. Parliamentary Papers
CBGN	Canada. Department of Mines and Resources/Department of Mines and Technical Surveys. Canadian Board on Geographical Names

CCGS	Canadian Coast Guard Ship
CLE	Crocker Land Expedition, 1913–17
CPCGN	Canada. Department of Mines and Technical Surveys/Department of Energy, Mines and Resources. Canadian Permanent Committee on Geographical Names
CRREL	United States Army. Cold Regions Research and Engineering Laboratory
DEMR	Canada. Department of Energy, Mines and Resources (now Natural Resources Canada)
DIAND	Canada. Department of Indian Affairs and Northern Development
DMR	Canada. Department of Mines and Resources (now Natural Resources Canada)
DMTS	Canada. Department of Mines and Technical Surveys (now Natural Resources Canada)
DND	Canada. Department of National Defence
DRB	Canada. Department of National Defence. Defence Research Board
EINPR	Canada. Environment Canada. Parks Service (now Canadian Heritage. Parks Canada). Ellesmere Island National Park Reserve
GBC	Canada. Geographic Board of Canada
GSC	Canada. Department of Mines and Technical Surveys/Department of Energy, Mines and Resources. Geological Survey of Canada
HMS	Her Majesty's Ship
IGY	International Geophysical Year, 1957–58
LFBE	United States. Army Signal Service. Lady Franklin Bay Expedition, 1881–84
OUELE	Oxford University Ellesmere Land Expedition, 1934–35
PCSP	Canada. Department of Energy, Mines, and Resources (now Natural Resources Canada). Polar Continental Shelf Project
RAF	Royal Air Force
RCAF	Royal Canadian Air Force
RCMP	Royal Canadian Mounted Police
RCN	Royal Canadian Navy
RM(A)(LI)	Royal Marine(s) (Artillery) (Light Infantry)
RN	Royal Navy
RNEIE	Royal Naval Expedition to Ellesmere Island, 1972
SS	Steamship
SY	Steam Yacht
USAF	United States Air Force
USCG(C)	United States Coast Guard (Cutter)
USN	United States Navy
USNR	United States Naval Reserve
USS	United States Ship
USNPE	United States. Department of the Navy. North Polar Expedition, 1871–73

The Geographical Names

ABBÉ GLACIER 82°01′N 71°30′W, flowing SE through the Garfield Range, was roughly mapped by the LFBE and named after Cleveland Abbé (1838–1916), a meteorologist with the U.S. Army Signal Service, 1871–91, and the U.S. Weather Bureau from 1891 (Greely, 1886, Vol. 1, map p. 390; DMR sheet 29^As½, 19^As½ and 9^As½, 1944; CBGN, 1960; DEMR sheet 120 F & 120 G, 1967; CPCGN, 1980:5).

ABBÉ RIVER 81°50′N 71°02′W, drains the *Abbé Glacier* (q.v.) and flows S into Lake Hazen; following field work from the DRB Hazen Camp in 1957–58, was so named in association with the glacier (CBGN, 1960; DEMR sheet 120 C & 120 D, 1967; CPCGN, 1980:5).

ADAMS GLACIER 81°38′N 74°19′W, flows SE from the main ice cap of northern Ellesmere Island, between Atka Lake and Mount Wiley; following field work from the DRB Hazen Camp in 1957–58, was so named in association with the *Adams River* (q.v.) (CBGN, 1960; Christie, 1962, Map 20; DEMR sheet 340 D, 1967; CPCGN, 1980:5).

ADAMS RIVER 81°38′N 73°02′W, flowing SE from Adams Glacier and then NE into the SW end of Lake Hazen, was roughly mapped by the LFBE in July 1882 and named probably after Captain William Adams, Master of the whaling ship *Arctic*, who in the 1870s had sailed N to the vicinity of Smith Sound (Greely, 1886, Vol. 1:393; DMR sheet 49^As½ and 39^As½, 1944; CBGN, 1960; Christie, 1962, Map 20; DEMR sheet 340 D, 1967; CPCGN, 1980:5).

AD ASTRA ICE CAP 81°36′N 74°19′W, at the head of Tanquary Fiord, following field work from the DRB Tanquary Camp in 1963–64, was so named from the motto of the RCAF, which supported DRB operations in northern Ellesmere Island (*Per Ardua Glacier*, q.v.) (CPCGN Decisions, 1965; DEMR sheet 340 D, 1967; CPCGN, 1980:5).

AGASSIZ ICE CAP 80°15′N 76°00′W, extending N towards the Dodge River and rising to c. 1400 m, was roughly mapped along its N front by the LFBE in May 1883 and named *Mer de Glace Agassiz*, after Louis Agassiz (1807–73), Swiss-born American zoologist and geologist; Professor of Natural History, University of Neuchâtel, 1832–46, and Professor of Zoology and Geology, Harvard University, 1848–73 (BA chart 275, 1885; Greely, 1886, Vol. 2:34 and map between p. 36 and 37; GBC Decisions, 1910; DMR sheet 49^As½ and 39^As½, 1944; DEMR sheet 340 D, 1967). *Agassiz Ice Cap* (CPCGN, 1980:6; DEMR sheet 340 D, 1988).

Agassiz, Mer de Glace: see Agassiz Ice Cap.

AIR FORCE GLACIER 81°41′N 76°30′W, flowing SSW from the main ice cap of northern Ellesmere Island towards the head of Tanquary Fiord, was sighted by the CLE in May 1915, when the name *Fiala Glacier* (q.v.) was applied probably to this feature (DMR sheet 49^As½ and 39^As½, 1944). Following field work from the DRB Gilman Glacier camp in 1957–58, the feature was named *Air Force Glacier* to mark a landing on the glacier by an RCAF DC-3 ski-wheel aircraft (CBGN,

1960; Christie, 1962, Map 20; DEMR
sheet 340 D, 1967; CPCGN, 1980:6).

AIR FORCE RIVER 81°30′N 76°42′W,
drains *Air Force Glacier* (q.v.) and flows
into the head of Tanquary Fiord;
following field work from the DRB
Tanquary Camp in 1962–63, was so
named in association with the glacier
(CPCGN Decisions, 1965; DEMR sheet
340 D, 1967; CPCGN, 1980:6).

Albert, Cape: see Albert Edward, Cape.

ALBERT EDWARD, CAPE 83°07′N
72°36′W, E entrance point of Disraeli
Fiord, was charted by the BAE in May
1876 and named after Albert Edward,
Prince of Wales (1841–1910), later
Edward VII, King of England, 1901–
10 (BA chart 275, 1877; BPP, 1877,
chart facing p. 172, p. 201; DMR sheet
49ᴬN½ and 39ᴬN½, 1944; CBGN, 1960;
DEMR sheet 340 E & 340 H, 1967;
CPCGN, 1980:7). *Cape Albert* (GBC,
1910:323).

ALDRICH, CAPE 83°06′N 69°35′W,
NW entrance point of Parr Bay, was
charted by the BAE in April-May 1876
and named after Lieutenant (later
Admiral) Pelham Aldrich, RN (1844–
1930), leader of the expedition's
western sledge party; Admiral
Superintendent, Portsmouth Dockyard,
1899–1902 (BA chart 275, 1877; BPP,
1877, chart facing p. 172; GBC,
1910:323; DMR sheet 29ᴬN½, 19ᴬN½
and 9ᴬN½, 1944; DEMR sheet 120 F &
120 G, 1967; CPCGN, 1980:7).

ALERT 82°30′N 62°22′W, on the W
side of Alert Inlet SSW of Cape
Belknap, was established by the
Canadian Meteorological Service and
the U.S. Weather Bureau as a Joint

Arctic Weather Station in August 1950,
and named after HMS *Alert* (Captain
G.S. Nares, RN), command ship of the
BAE (CBGN, 1949; DEMR sheet 120 E,
1966; CPCGN, 1980:1). The station was
established, and resupplied until 1962,
by USN and USCG icebreaker task
forces; since 1962, the station has been
completely supported by airlift, using
the aircraft runway (2 km N of the
station) on which construction was
started in 1950.

**ALERT, CANADIAN FORCES
STATION/ALERT, STATION DES
FORCES CANADIENNES** 82°30′N
62°20′W, on the W side of Alert Inlet,
was established in 1962 by the DND as
its farthest N military outpost (CPCGN
Decisions, 1966; DEMR sheet 120 E,
1988). The aircraft runway, situated
2 km N of the station on the NW side
of Dumbell Bay, is maintained by the
DND, and the station is completely
supported by airlift.

ALERT CREEK 82°29′N 62°18′W,
flows N into Alert Inlet, SE of the
station *Alert* (q.v.); following field
work by the Geographical Branch,
DMTS, in 1952, was so named in
association with the station (CBGN,
1953; DEMR sheet 120 E, 1966; CPCGN,
1980:7).

ALERT INLET 82°30′N 62°19′W, runs
NE-SW and forms the inner part of
Dumbell Bay, being joined by The
Narrows to the outer part of the bay;
following field work by the
Geographical Branch, DMTS, in 1952,
was so named in association with the
nearby station *Alert* (q.v.) (CBGN, 1953;
DEMR sheet 120 E, 1966; CPCGN,
1980:7).

ALERT, STATION DES FORCES CANADIENNES 82°30′N 62°20′W: see Alert, Canadian Forces Station.

ALEXANDRA, CAPE 83°03′N 74°39′W, W entrance point of Disraeli Fiord and NE point of Marvin Peninsula, was charted by the BAE in May 1876 and named after Alexandra, Princess of Wales (1844–1925), eldest daughter of Christian IX, King of Denmark, and later Queen Consort of Edward VII, King of England, 1901–10 (BA chart 275, 1877; BPP, 1877, chart facing p. 172, p. 201; GBC, 1910:323 and map; DMR sheet 49^A N½ and 39^A N½, 1944; CBGN, 1960; DEMR sheet 340 E & 340 H, 1967; CPCGN, 1980:8).

ALEXANDRA LAKE 81°46′N 65°32′W, draining SE into Musk-ox Bay, Discovery Harbour, was roughly charted by the BAE in 1875 and named *Lake Alexandra* after Alexandra, Princess of Wales *(Cape Alexandra,* q.v.) (BPP, 1877, chart facing p. 62; GBC, 1910:323; DMR sheet 29^A s½, 19^A s½ and 9^A s½, 1944). *Alexandra Lake* (CPCGN Decisions, 1969; CPCGN, 1980:8; DEMR sheet 120 C & 120 D, 1986).

Alexandra, Lake: see Alexandra Lake.

APPLEBY LAKE 81°51′N 68°16′W, near the head of Black Rock Vale and S of Kilbourne Lake, was roughly mapped by the LFBE in June 1882, and named *Lake Appleby* after Major Charles Appleby of New York, who assisted the expedition (Greely, 1886, Vol. 1:38, 372–373 and map p. 390). *Appleby Lake* (CBGN, 1960; DEMR sheet 120 C & 120 D, 1967; CPCGN, 1980:10).

Appleby, Lake: see Appleby Lake.

ARCHER FIORD 81°25′N 67°00′W, SW arm of Lady Franklin Bay between Keppel Head and Cape Baird, was charted by the BAE in April 1876 and named after Lieutenant (later Captain) Robert Hugh Archer, RN, (d. 1930) of HMS *Discovery*, who led a sledge party into the fiord (BA chart 275, 1877; BPP, 1877, chart facing p. 336; GBC, 1910, map; DMR sheet 29^A s½, 19^A s½ and 9^A s½, 1944; DEMR sheet 120 C & 120 D, 1967; CPCGN, 1980:11).

ARCTIC OCEAN/ARCTIQUE, OCÉAN surrounds the North Pole and is bounded by the northernmost coasts of Alaska, Canada, Greenland, Svalbard, and Russia, and is entered via the Chukchi Sea, Greenland Sea, or Barents Sea; was called the *Frozen Ocean* (Salmon, 1757:329); named *Arctic Ocean* (Arrowsmith, 1794, map; Brookes, 1826, map; Century Company, 1897, atlas, Map No. 3; Times, 1899, atlas, Maps 11–12; DEMR sheet 120 F & 120 G, 340 E & 340 H, 1967); also called *Polar Sea* by many 19th-century explorers (e.g., Hayes, 1867, book title; Nares, 1878, Vols. 1 and 2, book title; Nansen, 1897, Vol. 1:368) or *North Polar Sea* (BPP, 1877, chart facing p. 1). *Océan Arctique* (DEMR sheet 120 C & 120 D, 340 E & 340 H, 1988).

ARCTIQUE, OCÉAN: see Arctic Ocean.

ARROW GLACIER 81°52′N 72°04′W, flows SE from Blister Ice Cap, N of Bridge Glacier; following field work from the DRB Hazen Camp in 1957–58, was so named from its shape in plan (viewed from above) (CPCGN

Decisions, 1968; CPCGN, 1980:11; DEMR sheet 340 D, 1988).

ARROWHEAD MOUNTAIN 82°13'N 72°13'W, rises to c. 1860 m ENE of Mount Oxford; following field work from the DRB Gilman Glacier camp in 1957–58, was so named descriptively from its four main ridges rising to a sharp peak (CBGN, 1960; DEMR sheet 340 E & 340 H, 1967; CPCGN, 1980:11).

Arthur Eugene, Mount: see Eugene, Mount.

ARTHUR LAING PENINSULA 82°53'N 68°47'W, between Markham Fiord and Clements Markham Inlet, on the recommendation of DIAND was named after the Hon. Arthur Laing (1904–75), Minister of Northern Affairs and Natural Resources, 1963–66, Minister, DIAND, 1966–68, and Canadian Senator, 1972–75, in recognition of his services to Canada and, in particular, for his contribution to the development of the North (CPCGN Decisions, 1975; CPCGN, 1980:11; DEMR sheet 120 F & 120 G, 1987).

Arthur Land and Mountain: see Arthur, Mount.

ARTHUR, MOUNT 81°20'N 74°45'W, rising to c. 1295 m S of the head of the Very River, was roughly mapped and climbed by the LFBE in July 1882; named Mount C.A. Arthur after Chester Alan Arthur (1830–86), 21st President of the United States, 1881–85 (Vice President, 1880–81) (BA chart 275, 1885; Greely, 1886, Vol. 1, map p. 390, p. 399). *Mount Arthur* (Greely, 1886, Vol. 1:399, footnote; DMR sheet 49ᴬs½ and 39ᴬs½, 1944; CPCGN Decisions, 1968; CPCGN, 1980:11;

DEMR sheet 340 D, 1988). *Arthur Land and Mountain* [sic] (GBC, 1910:326).

ATKA LAKE 81°38'N 74°25'W, ice-dammed on the SW side of Adams Glacier, following field work from the DRB Hazen Camp in 1957–58, was named after the icebreaker USS *Atka* (Commander W.H. Reinhardt, USN), which in August 1958 reached the head of Chandler Fiord to evacuate the DRB party by helicopter (CPCGN Decisions, 1968; CPCGN, 1980:12; DEMR sheet 340 D, 1988).

Ayles Bay: see Ayles Fiord.

AYLES FIORD 82°45'N 80°00'W, between Cape Egerton and Cape Fanshawe Martin extending SE, was charted at its mouth by the BAE in May 1876 and named *Ayles Bay* after Petty Officer Adam Ayles, RN, Second Captain of Foretop in HMS *Alert* (BA chart 275, 1877; BPP, 1877, chart facing p. 172; GBC, 1910:327; DMR sheet 49ᴬs½ and 39ᴬs½, 1944). *Ayles Fiord* (CBGN, 1960; DEMR sheet 340 E & 340 H, 1967; CPCGN, 1980:13).

AYLES, MOUNT 82°43'N 77°18'W, rises to c. 1060 m on the W side of M'Clintock Inlet; following field work by the GSC in 1965, was named after Adam Ayles *(Ayles Fiord,* q.v.) (CPCGN Decisions, 1966; DEMR sheet 340 E & 340 H, 1967; CPCGN, 1980:13).

AYLES POINT 82°43'N 63°45'W, SW entrance point of Dana Bay, following survey by the BAE in September 1875, was named after Adam Ayles *(Ayles Fiord,* q.v.) (BPP, 1877, chart facing p. 78; GBC, 1910:327; CBGN, 1960; DEMR sheet 120 E, 1966; CPCGN, 1980:13).

BAIRD, CAPE 81°32'N 64°30'W, S entrance point of Lady Franklin Bay, was roughly charted by Hayes in May 1861 (Hayes, 1867, chart facing p. 72); charted by the USNPE in August 1871 (Davis, 1876:85); named by the USNPE, probably after Spencer Fullerton Baird (1823–87), American zoologist and Secretary, Smithsonian Institution, 1878–87; further charted by the BAE in April 1876 (BA chart 275, 1875; Ravenstein, 1875, map; BPP, 1877, chart facing p. 336; GBC, 1910, map; DMR sheet 29^{A}S½, 19^{A}S½ and 9^{A}S½, 1944; DEMR sheet 120 C & 120 D, 1967; CPCGN, 1980:14).

BARBEAU PEAK 81°55'N 75°02'W, highest peak in North America E of the Rocky Mountains, rises to 2505 m W of the head of Henrietta Nesmith Glacier; was climbed by a DRB-RAF field party from Gilman Glacier camp, 7 June 1967, when its height was determined (Hattersley-Smith, 1970:90–91); named after Dr. Marius Barbeau (1883–1969), Ethnologist, National Museum, Ottawa, 1911–48 (CPCGN Decisions, 1969; CPCGN, 1980:15; DEMR sheet 340 D, 1988).

BARRIER GLACIER 82°23'N 69°37'W, flows NW to form a barrier across the valley at the head of Clements Markham River; following field work from the DRB camp on Gilman Glacier in 1958, was so named descriptively (CBGN, 1960; DEMR sheet 120 F & 120 G, 1967; CPCGN, 1980:15).

BARRIER LAKE 82°23'N 69°46'W, is impounded by *Barrier Glacier* (q.v.) in the valley of Clements Markham River; following field work from the DRB camp on Gilman Glacier in 1958, was so named in association with the glacier (CBGN, 1960; DEMR sheet 120 F & 120 G, 1967; CPCGN, 1980:15).

Bartle-Frere, Mount: see Frere, Mount.

BEATRIX BAY 81°10'N 69°55'W, W arm of Archer Fiord and W of Record Point, was charted by the BAE in April 1876 and so named (BA chart 275, 1877; BPP, 1877, chart facing p. 336; DMR sheet 29^{A}S½, 19^{A}S½ and 9^{A}S½, 1944; DEMR sheet 120 C & 120 D, 1967; CPCGN Decisions, 1969; CPCGN, 1980:17).

BEAUFORT, MOUNT 81°54'N 63°30'W, rising to c. 400 m W of Cape Beechey, Robeson Channel, was sighted by Kane in June 1854 and named *Mount Francis Beaufort,* after Rear Admiral Sir Francis Beaufort (1774–1857), Hydrographer of the Royal Navy, 1829–55, and deviser of the Beaufort scale of wind force (Kane, 1856, Vol. 1, chart facing p. 5); charted by the USNPE in August 1871 and by the BAE in September 1875. *Mount Beaufort* (BA chart 275, 1875; Ravenstein, 1875, map; BPP, 1877, chart facing p. 38; DMR sheet 29^{A}S½, 19^{A}S½ and 9^{A}S½, 1944; DEMR sheet 120 C & 120 D, 1967; CPCGN Decisions, 1969; CPCGN, 1980:17). *Beaufort Mountain* (GBC, 1910:332).

Beaufort Mountain: see Beaufort, Mount.

BEECHEY, CAPE 81°54'N 63°04'W, marking the SW end of Black Cliffs, Robeson Channel, was sighted by Kane in June 1854 and named *Cape Beechy* [*sic*], after Rear Admiral Frederick William Beechey (1796–1856), Arctic explorer, who as a lieutenant served in HMS *Trent* (Commander John Franklin, RN) on

Buchan's expedition, 1818, and in HMS *Hecla* on Parry's expedition, 1819–20, and who commanded HMS *Blossom* on an expedition through Bering Strait to Point Barrow, 1825–28; President, Royal Geographical Society, 1855–56 (Kane, 1856, Vol. 1, chart facing p. 5); was charted by the USNPE in August 1871, and by the BAE in September 1875 and April 1876. *Cape Beechey* (BA chart 275, 1875; BPP, 1877, charts p. 38 and 116; GBC, 1910:332 and map; DMR sheet 29^As½, 19^As½ and 9^As½, 1944; DEMR sheet 120 C & 120 D, 1967; CPCGN, 1980:18).

Beechy, Cape: see Beechey, Cape.

BELKNAP, CAPE 82°31′N 62°11′W, N entrance point of Dumbell Bay, was sighted by the USNPE from the USS *Polaris* at c. 82°26′N in Robeson Channel, September 1871 (Davis, 1876:85); named by the USNPE after Major General William Worth Belknap (1829–90), a divisional commander in the Union forces during the American Civil War, 1861–65, and U.S. Secretary of War, 1869–76 (BA chart 275, 1877; BPP, 1877, chart facing p. 172; GBC, 1910, map; DMR sheet 29^AN½, 19^AN½ and 9^AN½, 1944; DEMR sheet 120 E, 1966; CPCGN, 1980:18); also called *Harley Spit* by the BAE after Petty Officer Daniel W. Harley, RN, Captain of Foretop in HMS *Alert* (BPP, 1877, chart facing p. 172).

Bellot, Cape: see Bellot Island.

BELLOT ISLAND 81°42′N 65°05′W, in the mouth of Discovery Harbour between Sun Cape and Distant Cape, was sighted by Kane in June 1854, and called *Cape Bellot,* after Lieutenant

Joseph René Bellot (1826–54), of the French Navy, who served on Franklin search expeditions to the Barrow Strait area in the *Prince Albert* (Captain W. Kennedy), 1850–51, and in HMS *Phoenix* (Captain E.A. Inglefield, RN), 1854, and who was drowned in Wellington Channel (Kane, 1856, Vol. 1, chart facing p. 5; BA chart 275, 1875; Ravenstein, 1875, map); charted by the BAE in September 1875 and named *Bellot Island* (BPP, 1877, chart facing p. 62; GBC, 1910:333 and map; DMR sheet 29^As½, 19^As½ and 9^As½, 1944; DEMR sheet 120 C & 120 D, 1967; CPCGN, 1980:19).

Bellows, The: see Bellows Valley, The.

Bellows Valley: see Bellows Valley, The.

BELLOWS VALLEY, THE 81°50′N 66°45′W, running SE to the W end of Discovery Harbour, was roughly charted by the BAE in October 1875 and named *The Bellows,* because of the persistent down-valley wind (BA chart 275, 1877; BPP, 1877:94 and chart facing p. 96; Greely, 1886, Vol. 1:93 and map p. 390; DMR sheet 29^As½, 19^As½ and 9^As½, 1944); *Bellows Valley* (Greely, 1886, Vol. 2:428; GBC, 1910:333). *The Bellows Valley* (CBGN, 1960; DEMR sheet 120 C & 120 D, 1967; CPCGN, 1980:19.

BENT GLACIER 81°19′N 78°16′W, flowing S into the NW side of Tanquary Fiord, was roughly mapped by the CLE in May 1915 and named after A.C. Bent, American ornithologist (GBC Decisions, 1928; DMR sheet 49^As½ and 39^As½, 1944; CPCGN Decisions, 1965; DEMR sheet 340 D, 1967; CPCGN, 1980:19).

Bethell Peak: see Bethel Peak.

BETHEL PEAK 82°54′N 78°55′W, rising to c. 650 m on the peninsula SE of Cape Richards, was charted by the BAE in May 1876 and named *Bethell* [*sic*] *Peak*, probably as a landmark after the ancient biblical city (BA chart 275, 1877; BPP, 1877, chart facing p. 172; DMR sheet 49^A½ and 39^AN½, 1944). *Bethel Peak* (CBGN, 1960; DEMR sheet 340 E & 340 H, 1967; CPCGN, 1980:20).

BEVERLEY, MOUNT 82°43′N 66°19′W, rising to c. 990 m on the SE side of Clements Markham Inlet, was charted by the BAE in April 1876 and called *Mount Wootton* after Commissioned Engineer James Wootton, RN, of HMS *Alert* (BPP, 1877, chart facing p. 172); later named *Mount Beverley* after Dr. Charles James Beverley (1788–1868), who as Surgeon RN and naturalist was a member of Ross's expedition in 1818 and of Parry's expedition, 1819–20, in search of the Northwest Passage (BA chart 275, 1877; GBC Decisions, 1910; DMR sheet 29^AN½, 19^AN½ and 9^AN½, 1944; DEMR sheet 120 F & 120 G, 1967; CPCGN, 1980:20). *Mount Beverly* [*sic*] (DEMR sheet 120 F & 120 G, 1988).

Beverley Point: see Hamilton Bluff.

Beverly, Mount: see Beverley, Mount.

BIEDERBICK LAKE 81°51′N 68°05′W, near the head of Black Rock Vale, was roughly mapped by the LFBE in June 1882 and named *Lake Biederbick* after Private Henry Biederbick, hospital steward and a survivor of the expedition (Greely, 1886, Vol. 1:373 and map p. 390). *Biederbick Lake* (CBGN, 1960; DEMR sheet 120 C & 120 D, 1967; CPCGN, 1980:10).

Biederbick, Lake: see Biederbick Lake.

BIEDERBICK, MOUNT 81°33′N 74°28′W, rising to c. 1430 m on the NE side of the Lewis River, was roughly mapped by the LFBE in July 1882 and named after Henry Biederbick *(Biederbick Lake,* q.v.) (BA chart 275, 1875; Greely, 1886, Vol. 1, map p. 390; GBC, 1910:334; DMR sheet 49^As½ and 39^As½, 1944; DEMR sheet 340 D, 1967; CPCGN, 1980:20).

BIRD POINT 82°52′N 65°16′W, NW entrance point of Sail Harbour, Parry Peninsula, was charted by the BAE in April 1876 and named after Lieutenant (later Admiral) Edward Joseph Bird, RN (1802–81), a member of Parry's expedition towards the North Pole from Spitsbergen in 1827 (BPP, 1877, chart facing p. 172; CBGN, 1960; DEMR sheet 120 F & 120 G, 1967; CPCGN, 1980:22).

BLACK CAPE 82°22′N 61°08′W, between Cape Union and Cape Rawson, Robeson Channel, was roughly charted by the USNPE from the USS *Polaris* in August 1871 (Davis, 1876:85); so named descriptively by the USNPE (BA chart 275, 1875; Ravenstein, 1875, map; BPP, 1877, chart facing p. 116; DMR sheet 29^AN½, 19^AN½ and 9^AN½, 1944; CBGN, 1953; DEMR sheet 120 E, 1966; CPCGN, 1980:22).

BLACK CLIFFS 81°57′N 62°47′W, running NE from Cape Beechey to Wrangel Bay, Robeson Channel, were charted by the BAE in September 1875 and so named descriptively (BA chart 275, 1877; BPP, 1877, chart facing p. 38; DMR sheet 29^As½, 19^As½ and 9^As½, 1944; DEMR sheet 120 C & 120 D, 1967; CPCGN, 1980:22).

BLACK CLIFFS BAY 82°32'N 62°50'W, between Cape Richardson and Cape Belknap, was sighted by the USNPE in September 1871 (Davis, 1876:85); called *Hilgard Bay* (q.v.) by the USNPE (Ravenstein, 1875, map), but this name was later restricted to the inner part of the bay; charted by the BAE in September 1875 and named descriptively *Black Cliffs Bay* (BA chart 275, 1877; BPP, 1877, chart facing p. 88; DMR sheet 29^{A}N½, 19^{A}N½ and 9^{A}N½, 1944; CBGN, 1953; DEMR sheet 120 E, 1966; CPCGN, 1980:22).

BLACK ROCK VALE 81°48'N 67°20'W, was roughly charted by the BAE in October 1875 and so named descriptively; further mapped by the LFBE (BA chart 275, 1877; BPP, 1877, chart facing p. 96; Greely, 1886, Vol. I, map p. 390; DMR sheet 29^{A}S½, 19^{A}S½ and 9^{A}S½2, 1944; CBGN, 1960; DEMR sheet 120 C & 120 D, 1967; CPCGN, 1980:22).

BLISTER CREEK 81°49'N 71°27'W, flows SE into Lake Hazen, just W of Hazen Camp; following field work from the camp in 1957–58, was so named because a member of the IGY party incurred a blister on his heel while walking up the creek (CBGN, 1960; DEMR sheet 120 C & 120 D, 1967; CPCGN, 1980:23).

BLISTER HILL 81°49'N 71°26'W, rises to c. 170 m just W of Hazen Camp; following field work from the DRB camp from 1962, was so named in association with *Blister Creek* (q.v.) (Savile, 1964, map p. 256–57; CPCGN, 1980:23; DEMR sheet 120 C & 120 D, 1986).

BLISTER ICE CAP 81°52'N 72°05'W, rises to c. 1200 m in the Garfield Range, WNW of Hazen Camp; following field work from the DRB camp in 1957–58, was so named in association with *Blister Creek* (q.v.), which drains the E part of the ice cap (CPCGN Decisions, 1968; CPCGN, 1980:23; DEMR sheet 340 D, 1988).

BORUP POINT 82°56'N 77°44'W, E of Bromley Island on the SW side of M'Clintock Inlet, following field work by the DRB-GSC-AFCRC group in 1954, was named after George Borup (1884–1912), of Yale University, a member of Peary's 1908–09 expedition, who supported the North Pole journey and who laid down a food cache W of this point; he was later drowned in a sailing accident off Portland, Maine (CBGN, 1960; DEMR sheet 340 E & 340 H, 1967; CPCGN, 1980:25).

BOULDER HILLS 82°12'N 67°12'W, rise to c. 1100 m S of Divide Glacier; following field work from the DRB Hazen Camp in 1957–58, were so named from their boulder-strewn surface (CBGN, 1960; DEMR sheet 120 F & 120 G, 1967; CPCGN, 1980:25).

BOWERY INLET 82°28'N 63°11'W, cove off W side of Black Cliffs Bay, following field work by the Geographical Branch, DMTS, in 1952, was named after Captain R.C.W. Bowery, of the Canadian Army, mentioned in dispatches, who lost his life in World War II (CBGN, 1953; DEMR sheet 120 E, 1966; CPCGN, 1980:25).

BOWMAN, MOUNT 81°21'N 76°30'W, rising to c. 1250 m SE of Tanquary Camp, was roughly mapped by the

CLE in May 1915 and named after Dr. Isaiah Bowman (1878–1950), Director, American Geographical Society, 1915–28, and President, Johns Hopkins University, 1928–50 (GBC Decisions, 1928; DMR sheet 49^A s ½ and 39^A s ½, 1944; DEMR sheet 340 D, 1967; CPCGN, 1980:26).

BREAKWATER ISLAND 81°42′N 64°45′W, off *Breakwater Point* (q.v.), Bellot Island, Lady Franklin Bay, was charted by the BAE in September 1875 and so named in association with the point (BA chart 275, 1877; BPP, 1877, chart facing p. 62; DEMR sheet 120 C & 120 D, 1967; CPCGN Decisions, 1969; CPCGN, 1980:26).

BREAKWATER POINT 81°42′N 64°47′W, forming a narrow E extension of Bellot Island, Lady Franklin Bay, was charted by the BAE in September 1875 and so named descriptively (BA chart 275, 1877; BPP, 1877, chart facing p. 62; DEMR sheet 120 C & 120 D, 1967; CPCGN Decisions, 1969; CPCGN, 1980:26).

BRIDGE GLACIER 81°51′N 72°08′W, flows ENE from Blister Ice Cap and forms a "bridge" between the heads of Ptarmigan Creek and Blister Creek; following field work from the DRB Hazen Camp in 1957–58, was so named descriptively (CBGN, 1960; DEMR sheet 340 D, 1967; CPCGN, 1980:27).

BRITISH EMPIRE RANGE 82°21′N 77°30′W, extends SW-NE between Yelverton Inlet and Disraeli Fiord, and rises to c. 2225 m at *Commonwealth Mountain* (q.v.); was sighted from the summit of *Mount Oxford* (q.v.) by the OUELE's northernmost sledge party and was so named by the leader of

that party, who was said to have been "a great imperialist" (Shackleton, 1937:256 and photo facing p. 262; DMR sheet 49^A N ½ and 39^A N ½, 1944; CBGN, 1960; DEMR sheet 340 E & 340 H, 1967; CPCGN, 1980:27).

BROMLEY ISLAND 82°56′N 78°18′W, forming the W entrance of M'Clintock Inlet, was charted as part of the mainland by the BAE in May 1876 (BPP, 1877, chart facing p. 172); following field work by the DRB-GSC-AFCRC group in 1954, named in association with *Bromley Peak* (q.v.) (CBGN, 1960; DEMR sheet 340 E & 340 H, 1967; CPCGN, 1980:27).

BROMLEY PEAK 82°57′N 78°15′W, rising to c. 400 m at the N end of Bromley Island, was charted by the BAE in May 1876 and named after Rear Admiral Arthur Charles Burgoyne Bromley (d. 1909), Lieutenant in HMS *Challenger* on the British deep-sea expedition, 1872–76 (BPP, 1877, chart facing p. 172; DMR sheet 49^A N ½ and 39^A N ½, 1944; CBGN, 1960; DEMR sheet 340 E & 340 H, 1967; CPCGN, 1980:27).

BULLEYS LUMP 81°11′N 69°15′W, rising to c. 780 m and forming the NE entrance point of Ella Bay, Archer Fiord, was charted by the BAE in April 1876 and named *Bulley's Lump* after Stoker Samuel Bulley, RN, of HMS *Discovery* (BPP, 1877, chart facing p. 336). *Bulleys Lump* (DMR sheet 29^A s ½, 19^A s ½ and 9^A s ½, 1944; DEMR sheet 120 C & 120 D, 1967; CPCGN Decisions, 1969; CPCGN, 1980:29).

Bulley's Lump: see Bulleys Lump.

BURKE BAY 81°08′N 78°42′W, NE of Cape Fernald, Tanquary Fiord, was roughly mapped by the CLE in May 1915 and named after E.I. Burke, American banker (GBC Decisions, 1928; DMR sheet 49^{As}½ and 39^{As}½, 1944; DEMR sheet 340 D, 1967; CPCGN, 1980:29).

CACHE CREEK 82°36′N 63°21′W, flows NE into Patterson Bay; following field work by the Geographical Branch, DMTS, in 1958, was so named from a cache laid in the vicinity (CBGN, 1959; DEMR sheet 120 E, 1966; CPCGN, 1980:30).

CAIRN BUTTE 82°31′N 62°14′W, on the SE side of Dumbell Bay, following field work by the Geographical Branch, DMTS, in 1958, was so named descriptively (CBGN, 1959; CPCGN, 1980:31; DEMR sheet 120 E, 1987).

CAMPBELL, MOUNT 81°42′N 65°05′W, highest point (c. 650 m) on Bellot Island, Lady Franklin Bay, was charted by the BAE in September 1875 and named possibly after Archibald Campbell, 1st Baron Blythswood (1835–1908), physicist and astronomer (BA chart 275, 1877; BPP, 1877, chart facing p. 62; DEMR sheet 120 C & 120 D, 1967; CPCGN Decisions, 1969; CPCGN, 1980:31).

CAPSTAN PEAK 82°17′N 78°15′W, rises to c. 1430 m S of the head of Milne Glacier; was climbed by the RNEIE in 1972 and so named descriptively (CPCGN Decisions, 1973; CPCGN, 1980:32; DEMR sheet 340 E & 340 H, 1988).

CAROLYN LAKE 81°17′N 70°44′W, SE of Dodge River, was mapped by the LFBE in May 1883 (Greely, 1886, Vol. 2, map between p. 36 and 37) and so

named by that expedition (BA chart 275, 1885; DMR sheet 29^{As}½, 19^{As}½ and 9^{As}½, 1944; DEMR sheet 120 C & 120 D, 1967; CPCGN Decisions, 1969; CPCGN, 1980:33).

CARTMEL POINT 81°48′N 63°47′W, NE entrance point of St. Patrick Bay, Robeson Channel, was charted by the BAE in September 1875 (BA chart 275, 1877; BPP, 1877, chart facing p. 116) and named after Senior Engineer Daniel Cartmel, RN, of HMS *Discovery* (DMR sheet 29^{As}½, 19^{As}½ and 9^{As}½, 1944; DEMR sheet 120 C & 120 D, 1967; CPCGN Decisions, 1969; CPCGN, 1980:33).

CHALLENGER MOUNTAINS 82°41′N 76°12′W, extending SW-NE from the head of Ayles Fiord to Disraeli Fiord and rising to c. 1400 m, were sighted by the BAE in May 1876 and named after HMS *Challenger,* commanded by Captain G.S. Nares, RN *(Cape Nares,* q.v.) ([extending from Yelverton Inlet to M'Clintock Inlet], BA chart 275, 1877; BPP, 1877, chart facing p. 172; GBC, 1910:343; DMR sheet 49^{A}½ and 39^{AN}½, 1944; [as now defined] DEMR sheet 340 E & 340 H, 1967; CPCGN, 1980:34).

Challenger, Point: see Stubbs Point.

Chandler Bay: see Chandler Fiord.

CHANDLER FIORD 81°38′N 68°46′W, NW arm of Conybeare Fiord, with Ruggles River at its head, was roughly mapped by the LFBE in April 1882 and named after William Eaton Chandler (1835–1917), Secretary of the U.S. Navy, 1882–85, responsible for fitting out and dispatching the relief expedition in

1884 (Greely, 1886, Vol. 1:267 and map p. 390; DMR sheet 29^{A}s½, 19^{A}s½ and 9^{A}s½, 1944; CBGN, 1960; DEMR sheet 120 C & 120 D, 1967; CPCGN, 1980:34). *Chandler Bay* (GBC, 1910:343).

CHAPMAN GLACIER 81°16′N 79°53′W, flowing SE into the head of McKinley Bay, Tanquary Fiord, was roughly mapped by the CLE in May 1915 and named after Dr. Frank Michler Chapman (1864−1945), Curator of Ornithology, American Museum of Natural History, New York, 1908−45 (GBC Decisions, 1928; DMR sheet 49^{A}s½ and 39^{A}s½, 1944; DEMR sheet 340 D, 1967; CPCGN, 1980:34).

CHARYBDIS GLACIER 81°39′N 75°15′W, flows SW from the main ice cap of northern Ellesmere Island and, with *Scylla Glacier* (q.v.), impounds Ekblaw Lake and blocks the Lewis River valley; following field work from the DRB Hazen Camp in 1957−58, was so named because there is no passage between the two glaciers, in allusion to Greek mythology (CBGN, 1960; Christie, 1962, Map 20; DEMR sheet 340 D, 1967; CPCGN, 1980:35).

CHEOPS, MOUNT 82°35′N 65°45′W, rising to c. 1280 m N of the upper James Ross River, was sighted by the BAE in April 1876; named after Cheops or Khufu (fl. 2680 BC), King of ancient Egypt for 23 years and builder of the great pyramid at Gizeh (BA chart 275, 1877; GBC Decisions, 1910; DMR sheet 29^{A}N½, 19^{A}N½ and 9^{A}N½, 1944; DEMR sheet 120 F & 120 G, 1967; CPCGN, 1980:35).

CHRISTIANSEN LAKE 81°02′N 70°10′W, SW of the head of Ella Bay,

Archer Fiord, following field work by the PCSP in 1977, was named after Frederik Thorlip Christiansen (d. 1884), Greenlander with the LFBE, who died at Cape Sabine (CPCGN Decisions, 1978; CPCGN, 1980:36; DEMR sheet 120 C & 120 D, 1988).

CHURCH PEAK 81°16′N 65°38′W, rising to 765 m NW of Cape Defosse, Kennedy Channel, was roughly charted by Hayes in May 1861 and named *Church's Monument* after Frederick Edwin Church (1826−1900), American landscape painter (Hayes, 1867, chart facing p. 72, p. 374). *Church Peak* (BA chart 275, 1875; Ravenstein, 1875, map; GBC Decisions, 1910; DMR sheet 29^{A}s½, 19^{A}s½ and 9^{A}s½, 1944; DEMR sheet 120 C & 120 D, 1967; CPCGN Decisions, 1969; CPCGN, 1980:36).

Church's Monument: see Church Peak.

CLAY ISLAND 81°55′N 69°05′W, near the E end of Lake Hazen off the mouth of Salor Creek, was roughly mapped by the LFBE in June 1982 (Greely, 1886, Vol. 1, map p. 390); following field work from the DRB Hazen Camp in 1957−58, named after Henry Clay, civilian with the U.S. Army Signal Service and a member of the Howgate expedition to West Greenland, 1880−81, who joined the LFBE at Godhavn but left the expedition in August 1881, returning from Fort Conger in the ss *Proteus* (CBGN, 1960; DEMR sheet 120 C & 120 D, 1967; CPCGN, 1980:36).

CLEAR, CAPE 81°38′N 65°56′W, E entrance point of Sun Bay and SW point of Sun Cape Peninsula, Lady Franklin Bay, was charted by the BAE and so named descriptively (BA chart 275, 1877; BPP, 1877, chart facing p. 62; DMR sheet 29^As½, 19^As½ and 9^As½, 1944; CPCGN Decisions, 1969; DEMR sheet 120 C & 120 D, 1967; CPCGN, 1980:36).

CLEAVES GLACIER 81°26′N 76°00′W, flowing SW from Viking Ice Cap towards the Macdonald River, was probably the glacier sighted by the CLE in May 1915 and named after Howard H. Cleaves, American naturalist (GBC Decisions, 1928; DMR sheet 49^As½ and 39^As½, 1944; DEMR sheet 340 D, 1967; CPCGN, 1980:37).

CLEMENTS MARKHAM GLACIER 82°18′N 70°20′W, flows NE towards the head of *Clements Markham Inlet* (q.v.); following field work from the DRB Gilman Glacier camp in 1958, was so named in association with the inlet (CBGN, 1960; DEMR sheet 120 F & 120 G, 1967; CPCGN, 1980:37).

CLEMENTS MARKHAM INLET 82°45′N 67°00′W, between Cape Colan and Cape Hecla extending SW, was charted by the BAE in April 1876 and named after Clements Robert (later Sir Clements) Markham (1830–1916), traveller, geographer, and historian, who served as a midshipman in HMS *Assistance* on the Franklin search expedition, 1850–51, commanded by Captain H.T. Austin, RN; a cousin of Commander A.H. Markham, RN *(Markham Fiord,* q.v.), he accompanied the BAE as far as Godhavn, Greenland; Secretary, 1863–88, and President, 1893–1905, Royal Geographical Society, and President, International Geographical Congress, 1894–99 (BA chart 275, 1877; BPP, 1877:168 and chart facing p. 172; GBC,

1910:346; CBGN, 1957; DEMR sheet 120 F & 120 G, 1967; CPCGN, 1980:37). *Markham Inlet* (Nares, 1878, Vol. 2:11; DMR sheet 29^AN½, 19^AN½ and 9^AN½, 1944).

CLEMENTS MARKHAM RIVER 82°38′N 68°40′W, flows NE into the head of *Clements Markham Inlet* (q.v.); following field work from the DRB Gilman Glacier camp in 1958, was so named in association with the inlet (CBGN, 1960; DEMR sheet 120 F & 120 G, 1967; CPCGN, 1980:37).

COBB RIVER 81°42′N 71°26′W, flowing NE and N into Lake Hazen, E of Dyas Island, was roughly mapped by the LFBE in June 1882; shown as entering the lake S of Dyas Island, and named probably after Frances Greely (née Cobb), mother of A.W. Greely (Greely, 1886, Vol. 1:385–86 and map p. 390; CPCGN Decisions, 1960; DEMR sheet 120 C & 120 D, 1967; CPCGN, 1980:37).

COLAN BAY 82°30′N 62°49′W, between Cape Woollen and Cape Jolliffe, Black Cliffs Bay, was charted by the BAE in September 1875; following field work by the Geographical Branch, DMTS, in 1952, named after Fleet Surgeon T. Colan *(Colan Cape,* q.v.) (CPCGN Decisions, 1963; DEMR sheet 120 E, 1966; CPCGN, 1980:38).

COLAN, CAPE 82°55′N 66°20′W, NW entrance point of Clements Markham Inlet, was charted by the BAE in April 1876 and used as the site of a food cache; named after Fleet Surgeon Thomas Colan, M.D., RN, of HMS *Alert* (BA chart 275, 1877; BPP, 1877:168 and chart facing p. 172; GBC, 1910:347 and map; DMR sheet 29^As½, 19^As½ and

9^{A}s½, 1944; DEMR sheet 120 F &
120 G, 1967; CPCGN, 1980:38).

COLUMBIA, CAPE 83°06′41″N
69°57′13″W, northernmost point of
Ellesmere Island, of Canada and of
North America, was reached by the
BAE, 1 May 1876, charted and so
named, Columbia being the poetical
name for North America (BA chart 275,
1877; BPP, 1877, chart facing p. 172;
Nares, 1878, Vol. 2:11; Greely, 1886,
Vol. 1:251–52; GBC, 1910:348 and map;
DMR sheet 29^{A}½, 19^{A}½ and 9^{A}½,
1944). The original charting showed
the northernmost point as NNE of
Mount Cooper Key (q.v.), where the
name was accordingly positioned on
subsequent maps and charts, even after
post-World War II mapping from air
photographs showed the northernmost
point as situated WSW of Mount
Cooper Key and c. 2 km W of *Cape
Aldrich* (q.v.) (DEMR sheet 120 F &
120 G, 1967; CPCGN, 1980:38).
Following detailed survey by the DND
in 1992, the name *Cape Columbia* was
repositioned on this northernmost
point (CPCGN Decisions, 1993; DEMR
sheet 120 F & 120 G, 1993).

COMMANDO PEAK 82°16′N
79°10′W, rises to c. 1580 m S of the
upper part of Milne Glacier; following
its first ascent by two Royal Marine
commandos of the RNEIE in 1972, was
named accordingly (CPCGN Decisions,
1973; CPCGN, 1980:38; DEMR sheet
340 E & 340 H, 1988).

COMMONWEALTH MOUNTAIN
82°24′N 76°45′W, the highest
mountain in the *British Empire Range*
(q.v.), rises to c. 2225 m W of
M'Clintock Glacier; following field
work from the DRB Gilman Glacier

camp in 1957–58, was so named in
association with the range (CBGN,
1960; DEMR sheet 340 E & 340 H,
1967; CPCGN, 1980:38); first climbed
by an RAF Expedition (Wing
Commander D. le R. Bird) to
Ellesmere Island in May 1967.

Conger Mountains: see Conger Range.

CONGER RANGE 81°33′N 75°18′W,
extends W-E from Air Force River to
Adams River, rises to c. 1550 m, and
includes Ad Astra Ice Cap, Viking Ice
Cap, Mount Beiderbick and Mount
Connell; was sighted by the LFBE in
June 1882 and named *Conger Mountains*
after E.H. Conger (*Fort Conger*, q.v.)
(Greely, 1886, Vol. 1:393, 400; GBC,
1910:348). *Conger Range* (DMR sheet
29^{A}s½, 19^{A}s½ and 9^{A}s½, 1944; CPCGN
Decisions, 1978; CPCGN, 1980:39;
DEMR sheet 340 D, 1988).

CONNELL, MOUNT 81°36′N
74°10′W, rising to c. 1250 m near the
terminus of Adams Glacier, was
roughly mapped by the LFBE in June
1882 and named after Private Maurice
Connell, of the Third Cavalry, U.S.
Army, a survivor of the expedition (BA
chart 275, 1885; Greely, 1886, Vol. 1,
map p. 390, p. 392; DMR sheet 29^{A}s½,
19^{A}s½ and 9^{A}s½, 1944; DEMR sheet
340 D, 1967; CPCGN, 1980:39). *Connell
Mountain* (GBC, 1910:348).

Connell Mountain: see Connell, Mount.

Conybeare Bay: see Conybeare Fiord.

CONYBEARE FIORD 81°34′N
67°35′W, running WSW from Lady
Franklin Bay with its entrance
between Keppel Head and Cape Clear,
was charted in its outer part by the

BAE in April 1876 and named *Conybeare Bay,* after Sub-Lieutenant (later Rear Admiral) Crawford James Markland Conybeare, RN (1854–1937), the youngest officer on the expedition, of HMS *Discovery* but also serving in HMS *Alert,* May-July 1876 (BA chart 275, 1877; BPP, 1877, chart facing p. 38; Nares, 1878, Vol. 1:333; GBC, 1910:348; DMR sheet 29^{A}s½, 19^{A}s½ and 9^{A}s½, 1944); mapped in its inner part by the LFBE in April 1882 and named *Conybeare Inlet* (Greely, 1886, Vol. 1, map p. 390). *Conybeare Fiord* (CBGN, 1960; DEMR sheet 120 C & 120 D, 1967; CPCGN, 1980:39).

Conybeare Inlet: see Conybeare Fiord.

COOPER KEY, MOUNT 83°06′N 70°21′W, rising to 665 m as the western of two peaks WSW of Cape Columbia, was roughly charted by the BAE on 1 May 1876, when the name *Cooper Key Mountains* was applied to the two peaks, after Admiral Sir Astley Cooper Key (1821–88), First Lord of the Admiralty, 1879–85 (BA chart 275, 1877; BPP, 1877, chart facing p. 172; GBC, 1910:349; DMR sheet 29^{A}N½, 19^{A}N½ and 9^{A}N½, 1944). *North Cooper Key Peak,* referring to the E peak (BPP, 1877:169). *Cooper Key Peak,* referring to the E peak (Nares, 1878, Vol. 2:18). The name *Mount Cooper Key* was later applied to the W peak (DEMR sheet 120 C & 120 D, 1967; CPCGN, 1980:39).

Cooper Key Mountains: see Cooper Key, Mount.

Cooper Key Peak: see Cooper Key, Mount.

CRACROFT, CAPE 81°23′N 64°39′W, between Cape Defosse and Cape

Lieber, Kennedy Channel, was sighted by Kane in June 1854 and named *Cape Sophia Cracroft* after Miss Sophia Cracroft (d. 1892), niece of Sir John Franklin and a staunch supporter of the Franklin search expeditions (Kane, 1856, Vol. 1, chart facing p. 5); sighted by Hayes in May 1861, and charted by the USNPE in August 1871 and by the BAE in September 1875. *Cape Cracroft* (BA chart 275, 1875; Ravenstein, 1875, map; BPP, 1877, chart facing p. 38; GBC Decisions, 1910; DMR sheet 29^{A}s½, 19^{A}s½ and 9^{A}s½, 1944; DEMR sheet 120 C & 120 D, 1967; CPCGN, 1980:41).

CRAIG LAKE 81°52′N 68°47′W, S of the NE end of Lake Hazen, draining into the lake via Salor Creek, was roughly mapped by the LFBE in June 1882 and named *Lake Craig* (Greely, 1886, Vol. 1:374 and map p. 390). *Craig Lake* (CBGN, 1960; DEMR sheet 120 C & 120 D, 1967; CPCGN, 1980:41).

Craig, Lake: see Craig Lake.

CRANSTONE PENINSULA 82°55′N 72°20′N, between Disraeli Fiord and Markham Fiord, following field work by the GSC in 1979, was named after Able Seaman George Cranstone, RN of HMS *Alert,* a member of the BAE sledge party in support of the western journey (CPCGN, 1980; DEMR sheet 340 E & 340 H, 120 F and 120 G, 1986).

CRASH POINT 82°42′N 76°13′W, on the E side of M'Clintock Inlet, S of Ootah Bay, following field work by the GSC in 1965, was so named because a Piper Supercub on charter crash-landed near the point (CPCGN Decisions, 1966; DEMR sheet 340 E & 340 H, 1967; CPCGN, 1980:41).

CRESCENT GLACIER 82°24′N 70°36′W, is situated to the NW of Clements Markham Glacier and flows NE and N; following field work from the DRB Gilman Glacier camp in 1961, was so named from its general shape in plan (CPCGN Decisions, 1962; DEMR sheet 120 F & 120 G, 1967; CPCGN, 1980:41).

CRESSWELL, CAPE 82°38′N 63°15′W, NW entrance point of Patterson Bay, was sighted by the USNPE in September 1871 (Davis, 1876:85); named by the USNPE probably after John Angel James Creswell [*sic*] (1828–91), U.S. Postmaster General, 1869–74; charted by the BAE in September 1875 (BA chart 275, 1875; Ravenstein, 1875, map; BPP, 1877, chart facing p. 172; GBC, 1910:350; DMR sheet 29^AN½, 19^AN½ and 9^AN½, 1944; DEMR sheet 120 E, 1966; CPCGN, 1980:41); also called *Simmons Point* by the BAE after J. Simmons (*Williams Island,* q.v.) (BPP, 1877, chart facing p. 88).

CROZIER ISLAND 82°52′N 64°25′W, in the entrance of James Ross Bay, was charted by the BAE in April 1876 and named after Captain Francis Rawdon Moira Crozier, RN (1796–1848), a member of Parry's Arctic expeditions, 1821–23, 1824–25, and 1827, in command of HMS *Terror* on James Clark Ross's Antarctic expedition, 1839–43, and on Franklin's Arctic expedition, 1845–48 (in command of the expedition on Franklin's death in 1847) (BA chart 275, 1877; BPP, 1877, chart facing p. 172; GBC Decisions, 1910; DMR sheet 29^AN½, 19^AN½ and 9^AN½, 1944; DEMR sheet 120 F & 120 G, 1967; CPCGN, 1980:42).

C.S. SMITH, MOUNT 81°18′N 73°29′W, rising to c. 1005 m on the N side of Dodge River, was roughly mapped by the LFBE in July 1882 and named possibly after Brigadier General Charles Sidney Smith (1843–1922), of the U.S. Army (Greely, 1886, Vol. I, map p. 390; DMR sheet 49^As½ and 39^As½, 1944; DEMR sheet 340 D, 1967; CPCGN Decisions, 1968; CPCGN, 1980:42).

CUESTA CREEK 81°53′N 70°13′W, flows SE into Lake Hazen ESE of Hazen Camp; following field work from the DRB camp in 1957–58, was so named from the landform in this locality (CBGN, 1960; DEMR sheet 120 C & 120 D, 1967; CPCGN, 1980:42).

DALY RIVER 81°13′N 65°52′W, on *Judge Daly Promontory* (q.v.) flowing NE, E, and S into Kennedy Channel WSW of Cape Defosse, was so named in association with the promontory (CBGN, 1960; DEMR sheet 120 C & 120 D, 1967; CPCGN, 1980:43).

DANA BAY 82°43′N 63°50′W, between Cape Delano and Ayles Point, forming the inner part of Porter Bay, was roughly charted by the BAE in September 1875, and called *Lawrence Bay* after Petty Officer Edwin Lawrence, RN, Gunner's Mate in HMS *Alert* (BPP, 1877, chart facing p. 88); later named *Dana Bay* presumably after James Dwight Dana (1813–95), American geologist and a member of the United States Exploring Expedition to the Antarctic, 1838–42 (Captain Charles Wilkes, USN); (Nares, 1878, Vol. 2:330; Blackadar, 1954, Map 53-10; CBGN, 1960; DEMR sheet 120 E, 1966; CPCGN, 1980:43).

DEAN HILL 82°26′N 62°10′W, rising to 390 m NE of *Mount Pullen* (q.v.), was mapped by the BAE and so named, probably in jocular reference to The Reverend H.W. Pullen (Nares, 1878, Vol. 2:367; CBGN, 1959; DEMR sheet 120 E, 1966; CPCGN, 1980:44); also called *The Dean* (Nares, 1878, Vol. 1:275).

Dean, The: see Dean Hill.

DEFOSSE, CAPE 81°14′N 65°36′W, S of Church Peak, Kennedy Channel, was sighted by Kane in June 1854 and named *Cape Romain Desfossés* (Kane, 1856, Vol. 1, chart facing p. 5); sighted by Hayes in May 1861 and named *Cape Desfossés* (Hayes, 1867, chart facing p. 72); charted by the USNPE in August 1871 and by the BAE in September 1875. *Cape Defossés* (Ravenstein, 1875, map). *Cape Defosse* (BA chart 275, 1875; BPP, 1877, chart facing p. 38; GBC, 1910, map; DMR sheet 29^As½, 19^As½ and 9^As½, 1944; DEMR sheet 120 C & 120 D, 1967; CPCGN Decisions, 1969; CPCGN, 1980:45).

Defossés, Cape: see Defosse, Cape.

DELANO, CAPE 82°43′N 63°38′W, N entrance point of Porter Bay, was sighted by the USNPE in September 1871 (Davis, 1876:85) and named probably after Amasa Delano (1763–1823), American sea captain and maritime explorer (BA chart 275, 1875; Ravenstein, 1875, map; DMR sheet 29^AN½, 19^AN½ and 9^AN½, 1944; CBGN, 1960; DEMR sheet 120 E, 1966; CPCGN, 1980:45); charted by the BAE in September 1875 and called *View Point* (BPP, 1877, chart facing p. 88) or *Delano Point* (BPP, 1877, chart facing p. 172).

Delano Point: see Delano, Cape.

DEPOT POINT 81°15′N 69°09′W, NE entrance Point of Simmons Bay, Archer Fiord, was charted by the BAE in April 1876 (BA chart 275, 1877; BPP, 1877, chart facing p. 336) and so named from a food cache left there (BPP, 1877, chart facing p. 38; CPCGN Decisions, 1969; CPCGN, 1980:45; DEMR sheet 120 C & 120 D, 1986).

Depot Point: see Richardson, Cape.

Desfossés, Cape: see Defosse, Cape.

de VRIES GLACIER 81°52′N 78°21′W, flowing W and NW into the E side of Yelverton Inlet, was named after Christiaan Dirk Steven de Vries (1941–79), a Dutch-born Canadian Arctic geologist, who died in a helicopter accident at Fort Smith, Northwest Territories (CPCGN Decisions, 1979; CPCGN, 1980:46; DEMR sheet 340 D, 1988).

Discovery Bay: see Discovery Harbour.

DISCOVERY, CAPE 83°00′N 77°24′W, NE entrance point of M'Clintock Inlet, was charted by the BAE in May 1876 and named after the BAE ship HMS *Discovery* (Captain H.F. Stephenson, RN) (BA chart 275, 1877; BPP, 1877, chart facing p. 172; DMR sheet 49^AN½ and 39^AN½, 1944; CBGN, 1960; DEMR sheet 340 E & 340 H, 1967; CPCGN, 1980:47. *Cape Stephenson* (BPP, 1877:205–06).

Discovery Harbor: see Discovery Harbour.

DISCOVERY HARBOUR 81°42′N 65°20′W, on the NW side of Lady Franklin Bay with entrances on either side of Bellot Island, between Sun Cape and Distant Cape, was reached by the BAE on 25 August 1875 and became winter quarters for HMS *Discovery*; was charted and named after the ship *Discovery Bay* (BPP, 1877:44; Nares, 1878, Vol. 1:114; GBC, 1910:356) or *Discovery Harbour* (BA chart 275, 1877; BPP, 1877:42 and chart facing p. 62; Nares, 1878, Vol. 1:114; DMR sheet 29^As½, 19^As½ and 9^As½, 1944; DEMR sheet 120 C & 120 D, 1967; CPCGN, 1980:47); used by the LFBE as the site for *Fort Conger* (q.v.). *Discovery Harbor* (Greely, 1886, Vol. 1:79 and map facing p. 87).

Disraeli Bay: see Disraeli Fiord.

DISRAELI CREEK 82°59'N 74°06'W, flows NE into Disraeli Fiord SE of Cape Alexandra; following field work by the DRB-GSC-AFCRC group in 1954, was so named in association with the fiord (CBGN, 1960; DEMR sheet 340 E & 340 H, 1967; CPCGN, 1980:47).

DISRAELI FIORD 82°44'N 73°23'W, extending SE from its entrance between Cape Alexandra and Cape Albert Edward, was charted in its outer part by the BAE in May 1876 and named *Disraeli Bay* after Benjamin Disraeli, 1st Earl of Beaconsfield (*Mount Disraeli,* q.v.) (BA chart 275, 1877; BPP, 1877, chart facing p. 172, p. 201; GBC, 1910:356 and map; DMR sheet 49^AN½ and 39^AN½, 1944). *Disraeli Fiord* (Christie, 1962, Map 20; DEMR sheet 340 E & 340 H, 1967; CPCGN, 1980:47).

DISRAELI GLACIER 82°27'N 72°50'W, flows N from the main ice cap of northern Ellesmere Island into the head of *Disraeli Fiord* (q.v.);

following field work from the DRB Gilman Glacier camp in 1957–58, was so named in association with the fiord (CBGN, 1960; Christie, 1962, Map 20; DEMR sheet 340 E & 340 H, 1967; CPCGN, 1980:47).

DISRAELI, MOUNT 82°53'N 67°37'W, rising to c. 950 m on Arthur Laing Peninsula, W of Mount Gladstone, was roughly charted by the BAE in April 1876 and named after The Right Honourable Benjamin Disraeli, 1st Earl of Beaconsfield (1804–81), Chancellor of the Exchequer, 1852, 1858–59, and 1866–68, and Prime Minister of England, 1868 and 1874–80 (BA chart 275, 1877; BPP, 1877, chart facing p. 172, p. 191; DMR sheet 29^As½, 19^As½ and 9^As½, 1944; CBGN, 1960; DEMR sheet 120 F & 120 G, 1967; CPCGN, 1980:47).

DISTANT CAPE 81°43'N 64°27'W, E entrance point of Discovery Harbour, Lady Franklin Bay, was charted by the BAE and so named as the farthest point visible to eastward from the harbour (BA chart 275, 1877; BPP, 1877, chart facing p. 62; Nares, 1878, Vol. 1:117; DMR sheet 29^As½, 19^As½ and 9^As½, 1944; CBGN, 1960; DEMR sheet 120 C & 120 D, 1967; CPCGN, 1980:47). *Cape Murchison* (q.v.), in error (BPP, 1877, chart facing p. 116).

DIVIDE GLACIER 82°15'N 67°25'W, flows S from Grant Ice Cap, N of Boulder Hills; following field work from the DRB Hazen Camp in 1957–58, was so named because meltwater from the glacier passes both northward via Piper Pass and southward via Lake Hazen (CBGN, 1960; DEMR sheet 120 F & 120 G, 1967; CPCGN, 1980:47).

DODGE RIVER 81°31′N 68°40′W, flowing NNE into Ida Bay, Conybeare Fiord, was roughly mapped by the LFBE in April 1882 and May 1883, when the name *Musk-ox Valley* was applied to its valley (BA chart 275, 1885; Greely, 1886, Vol. 1:62, Vol. 2:32−33 and map between p. 36 and 37); named *Dodge River,* possibly after Henry W. Dodge, Mate in Hayes' schooner *United States,* 1860−61 (BA chart 275, 1885; DMR sheets 29^A^S½, 19^A^S½ and 9^A^S½, 49^A^S½ and 39^A^S½, 1944; CBGN, 1960; DEMR sheets 120 C & 120 D, 340 D, 1967; CPCGN, 1980:47).

DOIDGE BAY 82°59′N 68°45′W, between Stubbs Point and Good Point, Arthur Laing Peninsula, was roughly charted by the BAE in April 1876 and named after Petty Officer James Doidge, RN, Captain of the Foretop in HMS *Alert* and a member of the sledge party at the time (BA chart 275, 1877; BPP, 1877, chart facing p. 172, p. 195; GBC, 1910:357; DMR sheet 29^A^N½, 19^A^N½ and 9^A^N½, 1944; DEMR sheet 120 F & 120 G, 1967; CPCGN, 1980:48).

DRYAS GLACIER 82°20′N 71°00′W, flows SE from Seven Sisters Peaks into the valley of the Gilman River; following field work from the DRB Hazen Camp in 1957−58, was so named from the arctic avens *(Dryas integrifolia)* plentiful in the valley (CBGN, 1960; DEMR sheet 120 C & 120 D, 1967; CPCGN, 1980:49).

Dumb Bell Bay: see Dumbell Bay.

Dumb Bell Lakes: see Lower Dumbell Lake or Upper Dumbell Lake.

DUMBELL BAY 82°31′N 62°15′W, between Cape Belknap and Sickle Point, with The Narrows between the outer part and the inner part (*Alert Inlet,* q.v.) of the bay, was charted by the BAE in September 1875 and named from its shape *Dumb Bell Bay* (BA chart 275, 1877; BPP, 1877, chart facing p. 126; DMR sheet 29^A^N½, 19^A^N½ and 9^A^N½, 1944). *Dumbell Bay* (CBGN, 1953; DEMR sheet 120 E, 1966; CPCGN, 1980:50).

DUMBELL CREEK 82°29′N 62°46′W, flowing W from Lower Dumbell Lake to the E shore of Colan Bay, was so named in association with the lake (CPCGN Decisions, 1962; CPCGN, 1980:50; DEMR sheet 120 E, 1988).

DYAS ISLAND 81°42′N 71°53′W, off the S shore and towards the W end of Lake Hazen, was roughly mapped by the LFBE in June 1882 and so named, possibly in error for arctic avens (*Dryas integrifolia*) found growing there (Greely, 1886, Vol. 1:389 and map p. 390; DMR sheet 29^A^S½, 19^A^S½ and 9^A^S½, 1944; DEMR sheet 120 C & 120 D, 1967; CPCGN, 1980:51).

EASTWIND BAY 81°35′N 67°46′W, on the N side of Conybeare Fiord, was named after the icebreaker USCGC *Eastwind* (Captain R.F. Rae, USCG), which anchored in nearby Chandler Fiord during the relief of the DRB Hazen Camp in August 1957 (CBGN, 1960; DEMR sheet 120 C & 120 D, 1967; CPCGN, 1980:52).

Edward Parry, Mount: see Parry, Mount.

EGERTON CREEK 82°30′N 63°08′W, drains *Egerton Lake* (q.v.) NE into Black Cliffs Bay; following field work by the Geographical Branch, DMTS, in 1952, was so named in association with the lake (CBGN, 1953; CPCGN, 1980:52; DEMR sheet 120 E, 1987).

EGERTON LAKE 82°29'N 63°20'W, W of Bowery Inlet, Black Cliffs Bay, following field work by the Geographical Branch, DMTS, in 1952, was named after Admiral Sir George (le Clerc) Egerton (1852–1940), Sub-Lieutenant in HMS *Alert* of the BAE, later Second Sea Lord of the Admiralty, 1911–12, and Commander-in-Chief, Plymouth, 1913–16 (CBGN, 1953: DEMR sheet 120 E, 1966; CPCGN, 1980:52).

EGINGWAH BAY 82°46'N 76°56'W, on the W side of M'Clintock Inlet, following field work by the GSC in 1965, was named after the Inughuit dog-driver Egingwah, from the Thule District, North Greenland, a member of Peary's teams that travelled the whole north coast of Ellesmere in 1906 and that reached the North Pole in 1909 (*Ootah Bay,* q.v.) (CPCGN Decisions, 1966; DEMR sheet 340 E & 340 H, 1967; CPCGN, 1980:53).

EGINGWAH CREEK 82°47'N 77°00'W, flows E into *Egingwah Bay* (q.v.), M'Clintock Inlet; following field work by the GSC in 1965, was so named in association with the bay (CPCGN Decisions, 1966; DEMR sheet 340 E & 340 H, 1967; CPCGN, 1980:53).

EKBLAW LAKE 81°40'N 75°40'W, is impounded by the Scylla and Charybdis Glaciers to the NE of Ad Astra Ice Cap; following field work from the DRB Hazen Camp in 1957–58, was named after Walter Elmer Ekblaw (1882–1949), geologist and botanist on the CLE, who discovered Tanquary Fiord in May 1915 (CBGN,

1960; Christie, 1962, Map 20; DEMR sheet 340 D, 1967; CPCGN, 1980:53).

ELLA BAY 81°07'N 69°50'W, SW arm of Archer Fiord between Record Point and Bulleys Lump, was charted by the BAE in April 1876 and so named (BA chart 275, 1877; BPP, 1877, chart facing p. 336; DMR sheet 29^As½, 19^As½ and 9^As½, 1944; DEMR sheet 120 C & 120 D, 1967; CPCGN Decisions, 1969; CPCGN, 1980:53).

ELLESMERE, ÎLE D' 79°30'N 76°00'W: see Ellesmere Island.

ELLESMERE ISLAND/ELLESMERE, ÎLE D' 79°30'N 76°00'W, extends N-S from the Arctic Ocean at Cape Columbia to Jones Sound. The SE coast of the island was roughly charted by Inglefield in September 1852, when the name *Ellesmere Island* was applied to the unexplored hinterland of the W coast of Smith Sound, after Francis Egerton, 1st Earl of Ellesmere (1800–57), English Statesman and poet, Secretary at War, 1839, President of the British Association, 1842, and Vice President, 1851–53, and President 1853–55, of the Royal Geographical Society (Inglefield, 1853, end chart). This hinterland was later called *Ellesmere Land* (Hayes, 1867, chart facing p. 72; Ravenstein, 1875, map; Nares, 1878, Vol. 1:48; Sverdrup, 1904, Vol. 1:28; Vol. 2, end map; Vibe, 1948, end map). Following definition of the insularity of the island by the Second Norwegian Polar Expedition in the *Fram* (Captain O. Sverdrup), the name *Ellesmere Island* was applied to the whole island, and the territorial names *Ellesmere Land, Grinnell Land* (q.v.) and *Grant Land* (q.v.) were rescinded (GBC

38

Decisions, 1904; GBC, 1910, map; CPCGN, 1980:53). Canadian Government maps used the new terminology, although until World War II some publications used the name *Ellesmere Land* to refer to the whole island (e.g., Shackleton, 1937, book subtitle and p. 23).

ELLESMERE ISLAND NATIONAL PARK RESERVE/ÎLE-D'ELLES-MERE, RÉSERVE DE PARC NATIONAL DE L' 82°13′N 72°13′W, has boundaries delineated on DEMR sheets 120 C & 120 D, 120 E, 120 F & 120 G, 340 D, and 340 E & 340 H, 1988. The park was formally established by order-in-council in 1986, and was included under the National Parks Act in 1988 (CPCGN Decisions, 1989; EINPR, 1991).

Ellesmere Land: see Ellesmere Island.

EUGENE GLACIER 82°16′N 66°35′W, flows SE from Grant Ice Cap, NE of Boulder Hills; following field work by a DRB-GSC field party from Alert in 1953, was so named in association with *Mount Eugene* (q.v.) to the N (CBGN, 1959; DEMR sheet 120 F & 120 G, 1967; CPCGN, 1980:56).

EUGENE, MOUNT 82°25′N 66°47′W, rising to c. 1850 m above Grant Ice Cap, United States Range, was sighted by the LFBE in July 1883 and named *Mount Arthur Eugene* (Greely, 1888, Vol. 1:319); following field work from the DRB Hazen Camp in 1957–58, named *Mount Eugene* (CBGN, 1959; DEMR sheet 120 F & 120 G, 1967; CPCGN, 1980:56).

FEILDEN PENINSULA 82°47′N 63°50′W, between James Ross Bay and Porter Bay, terminating in Cape Joseph Henry, was sighted by the USNPE in

September 1871 (Davis, 1876:85); charted by the BAE in April 1876 and named after Captain (later Colonel) Henry Wemyss Feilden, Royal Artillery (1832–1921), naturalist in HMS *Alert*, who had previously served in the Confederate Army in the American Civil War, 1862–65 (BA chart 275, 1877; BPP, 1877, chart facing p. 172; GBC, 1910:367; DMR sheet 29ᴬN½, 19ᴬN½ and 9ᴬN½, 1944; DEMR sheet 120 E, 1966; CPCGN, 1980:58).

FERBRACHE PENINSULA 82°43′N 80°40′W, between Milne Fiord and Ayles Fiord extending NW to Cape Egerton, following field work by the GSC in 1979, was named after Able Seaman William Ferbrache, RN, of HMS *Alert* on the BAE (CPCGN, 1980; DEMR sheet 340 E & 340 H, 1988).

FERNALD, CAPE 81°07′N 78°37′W, NE entrance point of McKinley Bay, Tanquary Fiord, was roughly mapped by the CLE in May 1915 and named after Dr. Merritt Lyndon Fernald (1873–1950), Professor of Natural History, Harvard University, 1915–49 (GBC Decisions, 1928; DMR sheet 49ᴬs½ and 39ᴬs½, 1944; DEMR sheet 340 D, 1967; CPCGN, 1980:58).

FIALA GLACIER 81°39′N 76°45′W, flowing ESE to abut *Air Force Glacier* (q.v.) at the head of Air Force River, was roughly mapped by the CLE in May 1915 and named (the name was probably first applied to the other glacier, but later transferred to the present feature) after Anthony Fiala (1871–1950), Commander of the U.S. Ziegler Polar Expedition, 1903–05, to Franz Josef Land (Zemlya Frantsa Iosifa) (GBC Decisions, 1928; CPCGN, 1980:58; DEMR sheet 340 D, 1988).

Fiala Glacier: see Air Force Glacier.

FISHHOOK POINT 81°19'N 77°35'W, on the SE side of Tanquary Fiord, following field work from the DRB camp in 1963–64, was so named from its outline in plan (CPCGN Decisions, 1967; CPCGN, 1980:59; DEMR sheet 340 D, 1988).

FLOEBERG BEACH 82°27'N 61°25'W, extending NW-SE from Cape Sheridan to Cape Rawson, was charted by the BAE in September 1875 and so named from the massive floes of multiyear sea ice ("floebergs") grounded off the beach (Nares, 1878, Vol. 1:138; CBGN, 1960; DEMR sheet 120 E, 1966; CPCGN, 1980:60).

FORK MOUNTAIN 82°20'N 71°39'W, rises to 2105 m NW of the head of Crescent Glacier; following field work from the DRB Gilman Glacier camp in 1961, was so named from the conspicuous "fork" formed by two rock ridges on the S face (CPCGN Decisions, 1962; DEMR sheet 120 F & 120 G, 1967; CPCGN, 1980:6).

FORT CONGER 81°45'N 64°45'W, on the E shore of Discovery Harbour, Lady Franklin Bay, was the winter station established by the LFBE in August 1881 and named after Edwin Hurd Conger (1843–1907), U.S. Senator and diplomat, who assisted the expedition (Greely 1886, Vol. 1:84, map facing p. 87, p. 90, Vol. 2, front.; DMR sheet 29ᴬs½, 19ᴬs½ and 9ᴬs½, 1944; CPCGN Decisions, 1960; DEMR sheet 120 C & 120 D, 1967; CPCGN, 1980:2). HMS *Discovery* of the BAE had wintered close offshore in 1875–76, and in 1899 Peary dismantled the LFBE hut to construct three small huts,

which were also used by later expeditions, including the CLE, the Third Thule Expedition to Cape Columbia in 1920, Lauge Koch's Greenland expedition in 1921, and the OUELE (Hattersley-Smith, 1964b; Dick, 1991).

FOSTER, MOUNT 82°52'N 66°58'W, rising to c. 950 m SW of Cape Colan, was charted by the BAE in April 1876 (BPP, 1877:193) and named after Commander Henry Foster, RN (1796–1831), polar explorer, navigator, and astronomer; he served on Parry's Arctic expeditions, 1824–25 and 1827, and commanded HMS *Chanticleer* on the naval scientific expedition to the South Atlantic region, 1828–31, where he made discoveries in the South Shetland Islands and on the Antarctic Peninsula; on the return voyage he was drowned in the Chagres River, Panama, in February 1831, after an affray with natives (BA chart 275, 1877; Nares, 1878, Vol. 1, chart facing p. 1; DMR sheet 29ᴬN½, 19ᴬN½ and 9ᴬN½, 1944; CBGN, 1960; DEMR sheet 120 F & 120 G, 1967; CPCGN, 1980:61).

FREDERICK VII, CAPE 82°06'N 61°55'W, SW entrance point of Lincoln Bay on Robeson Channel, was sighted by Hayes in May 1861 and named after Frederick VII (1808–63), King of Denmark, 1848–63, "to whose subjects in Greenland I am indebted for so many serviceable attentions"; charted by the BAE in September 1875 and April 1876 (Hayes, 1867, chart facing p. 72, p. 374; BA chart 275, 1875; BPP, 1877, chart facing p. 116; GBC, 1910:368; DMR sheet 29ᴬN½, 19ᴬN½ and 9ᴬN½, 1944; DEMR sheet 120 E, 1966; CPCGN, 1980:62).

Frere, Mount c. 82°37′N 70°25′W, rising to c. 1500 m W of the head of Clements Markham Inlet, was roughly charted by the BAE in April 1876 and named *Mount Frere*, after Sir (Henry) Bartle (Edward) Frere, 1st Baronet (1815–84), British statesman, Governor of Bombay, 1862–67, and Governor of Cape of Good Hope, 1877–80; President, Royal Geographical Society, 1872–73 (BA chart 275, 1877; Nares, 1878, Vol. 1, chart facing p. 1; DMR sheet 29^{A}N½, 19^{A}N½ and 9^{A}N½, 1944). *Mount Bartle-Frere* (Nares, 1878, Vol. 1:325). *Frere Mountain* (GBC Decisions, 1910). The name was later rescinded for lack of positive identification (CBGN, 1960).

Frere Mountain: see Frere, Mount.

Frozen Ocean: see Arctic Ocean.

GABLE CLIFF 82°48′N 65°15′W, along the E side of Parker Bay, Parry Peninsula, was charted by the BAE in April 1876 and so named descriptively (BPP, 1877, chart facing p. 172; CBGN, 1960; DEMR sheet 120 F & 120 G, 1967; CPCGN, 1980:63).

GAP MOUNTAIN 82°39′N 64°35′W, rising to c. 925 m SW of Porter Bay, was charted by the BAE in April 1876 and so named as a landmark seen through a gap in the coastal hills (BA chart 275, 1877; BPP, 1877, chart facing p. 126; DMR sheet 29^{A}N½, 19^{A}N½ and 9^{A}N½, 1944; CBGN, 1960; DEMR sheet 120 F & 120 G, 1967; CPCGN, 1980:63).

Garfield Mountains: see Garfield Range.

GARFIELD RANGE 81°48′N 72°40′W, extends SW-NE from Turnstone Glacier to Gilman Glacier on the NW side of Lake Hazen, rises to c. 1400 m, and includes McGill, Omingmak, and Varsity Mountains; was roughly mapped by the LFBE in 1882 and named after James Abram Garfield (1831–81), 20th President of the United States, 1880–81, until he was assassinated (BA chart 275, 1885; Greely, 1886, Vol. 1:276, 393; GBC, 1910:369; [extending SW-NE from Adams River to Eugene Glacier] DMR sheets 49^{A}s½ and 39^{A}s½, 29^{A}N½, 19^{A}N½ and 9^{A}N½, 1944, [as now defined] CBGN, 1960; Christie, 1962, Map 20; DEMR sheets 340 D, 120 C & 120 D, 120 F & 120 G, 1967; CPCGN, 1980:63). *Garfield Mountains* (Greely, 1886, Vol. 1, map p. 390).

GATTER ISLAND 81°55′N 69°06′W, near the E end of Lake Hazen off the mouth of Salor Creek, was roughly mapped by the LFBE in June 1882 and so named (Greely, 1886, Vol. 1, map p. 390; DMR sheet 29^{A}s½, 19^{A}s½ and 9^{A}s½, 1944; CBGN, 1960; DEMR sheet 120 C & 120 D, 1967; CPCGN, 1980:64).

GIFFARD BAY 82°30′N 61°52′W, between Mushroom Point and Mann Point, was charted by the BAE in September 1875 (BPP, 1877, chart facing p. 88); named after Lieutenant G.A. Giffard (*Giffard Peak*, q.v.) (CBGN, 1953; CPCGN, 1980:65; DEMR sheet 120 E, 1988).

GIFFARD PEAK 82°58′N 68°20′W, rising to c. 790 m SE of Good Point, Arthur Laing Peninsula, was roughly charted by the BAE in April 1876 and named after Lieutenant (later Admiral) George Augustus Giffard, RN (1849–1925), Third Lieutenant in HMS *Alert*, who supported the western sledge journey; Admiral Superintendent, HM Dockyard, Chatham, 1907–09 (BA chart 275, 1877; BPP, 1877, chart facing p. 172, p. 193; DMR sheet 29ᴬN½, 19ᴬN½ and 9ᴬN½, 1944; CBGN, 1960; DEMR sheet 120 F & 120 G, 1967; CPCGN, 1980:65). *Giffard Point*, in error (GBC, 1910:370).

Giffard Point: see Giffard Peak.

GILMAN GLACIER 82°07′N 70°45′W, flowing SE from the main ice cap of northern Ellesmere Island towards Lake Hazen, was roughly mapped by the LFBE in June 1882 and named after Professor Daniel Colt Gilman (1831–1908), first President, Johns Hopkins University, Baltimore, 1875–1901, who supported the scientific work of the expedition (BA chart 275, 1885; Greely, 1886, Vol. 1, map p. 390, p. 409; Shackleton, 1937:252–53 and end map; DMR sheet 29ᴬN½, 19ᴬN½ and 9ᴬN½, 1944; CBGN, 1960; DEMR sheet 120 F & 120 G, 1967; CPCGN, 1980:65). The glacier was the site of DRB summer camps between 1957 and 1967 (Hattersley-Smith, 1974:44–47, 52–56, 62–64).

GILMAN RIVER 81°56′N 69°27′W, drains *Gilman Glacier* (q.v.) and flows SE into the E end of Lake Hazen; following field work from the DRB camp on the glacier in 1957–58, was so named in association with the glacier (CBGN, 1960; DEMR sheet 120 C & 120 D, 1967; CPCGN, 1980:65).

GLACIER PASS 81°56′N, 71°39′W, runs NE-SW between the Abbé River and the Snow Goose River, SE of Roundel Glacier, and rises to c. 920 m; following field work from the DRB

Hazen Camp in 1957–58, was so named descriptively (CBGN, 1960; DEMR sheet 120 C & 120 D, 1967; CPCGN, 1980:65).

GLADSTONE, MOUNT 82°53′N 67°16′W, rising to c. 930 m E of Mount Disraeli, Arthur Laing Peninsula, was roughly charted by the BAE in April 1876 and named after The Right Honourable William Ewart Gladstone (1809–98), Chancellor of the Exchequer, 1852–55 and 1859–66, and Prime Minister of England, 1868–74, 1880–85, 1886, and 1892–94 (BA chart 275, 1877; BPP, 1877, chart facing p. 172, p. 191; DMR sheet 29ᴬS½ and 9ᴬS½, 1944; CBGN, 1960; DEMR sheet 120 F & 120 G, 1967; CPCGN, 1980:66).

GLEASON, CAPE 81°10′N 78°25′W, on the E side of Tanquary Fiord, was roughly mapped by the CLE in May 1915 and named after Henry Allen Gleason, American botanist, New York Botanical Garden (GBC Decisions, 1928; DMR sheet 49ᴬS½ and 39ᴬS½, 1944; DEMR sheet 340 D, 1967; CPCGN, 1980:66).

GOOD POINT 83°01′N 68°30′W, E entrance point of Doidge Bay, Arthur Laing Peninsula, was mapped by the BAE in April 1876 and named after Chief Petty Officer James Good, RN, Chief Boatswain's Mate in HMS *Alert* (BA chart 275, 1877; BPP, 1877, chart facing p. 172; GBC, 1910:371; DMR sheet 29ᴬS½, 19ᴬS½ and 9ᴬS½, 1944; DEMR sheet 120 F & 120 G, 1967; CPCGN, 1980:66). *Point Good* (BPP, 1877:195).

Good, Point: see Good Point.

GRANT ICE CAP 82°25'N 66°45'W, extends E and NE from Piper Pass to the headwaters of the Wood River and James Ross River, and rises to c. 1700 m; was so named in association with *Mount Grant* (q.v.) (CBGN, 1959; DEMR sheet 120 F & 120 G, 1967; CPCGN, 1980:68).

Grant Land c. 82°00'N 64°00'W, formerly unexplored hinterland W of Robeson Channel, was sighted by the USNPE in August 1871 and named after Ulysses S. Grant (*Mount Grant*, q.v.) (Ravenstein, 1875, map; Davis 1876, map between p. 356–57; BA chart 275, 1877; BPP, 1877, chart facing p. 1; Nares, 1878, Vol. 1:109; Greely, 1886, Vol. 1, map p. 305; Vibe, 1948, end map), but the name was later rescinded for official use (GBC, 1910:372).

GRANT, MOUNT 82°27'N 65°55'W, rising to c. 1580 m on the NE side of Grant Ice Cap, was roughly charted by the BAE in April 1876 and, in association with the former name *Grant Land* (q.v.), was named after General Ulysses Simpson Grant (1822–85), Commander-in-Chief of the Union Army in the American Civil War, 1861–65, and 18th President of the United States, 1869–77 (BA chart 275, 1877; BPP, 1877, chart facing p. 172; GBC, 1910:372; DMR sheet 29^AN½, 19^AN½ and 9^AN½, 1944; CBGN, 1960; DEMR sheet 120 F & 120 G, 1967; CPCGN, 1980:68); first climbed by a DRB-GSC party in July 1953 (Hattersley-Smith, 1974:28).

GRANT RIVER 82°26'N 65°16'W, drains glaciers SE of *Mount Grant* (q.v.) and flows NE to join the Wood River; following field work by the Geographical Branch, DMTS, in 1958, was so named in association with the

mountain (CBGN, 1959; DEMR sheet 120 F & 120 G, 1967; CPCGN, 1980:68).

GREEN VALLEY 81°25'N 76°48'W, runs NE-SW from the head of May Creek to the head of Yellowstone Creek, S of Tanquary Camp; following field work from the DRB camp in 1967–68, was so named because this sheltered upland valley, containing two shallow ponds, is surprisingly well vegetated (CPCGN Decisions, 1971; CPCGN, 1980:69; DEMR sheet 340 D, 1988).

Grinnell Land c. 81°00'N 70°00'W, formerly unexplored hinterland W of Kennedy Channel, was sighted by Kane in June 1854 and named after Henry Grinnell (*Mount Grinnell*, q.v.) (Kane, 1856, Vol. 1, chart facing p. 5; Hayes, 1867, chart facing p. 72; BA chart 275, 1875; Ravenstein, 1875, map; BPP, 1877, chart facing p. 38; Nares, 1878, Vol. 1:74; Greely, 1886, Vol. 1:74 and map p. 390; Vibe, 1948, end map), but the name was later rescinded for official use (*Ellesmere Island*, q.v.) (GBC, 1910:372).

GRINNELL, MOUNT 81°31'N 66°56'W, rises to 850 m above Keppel Head, Lady Franklin Bay; following a probable sighting by Kane in July 1854, was named after Henry Grinnell (1799–1874), American merchant and philanthropist, who sponsored Kane's Second Grinnell Expedition, 1853–55; charted by the BAE in April 1876 (BA chart 275, 1875; Ravenstein, 1875, map; BPP, 1877, chart facing p. 38; GBC, 1910:374; DMR sheet 29^As½, 19^As½ and 9^As½, 1944; DEMR sheet 120 C & 120 D, 1967; CPCGN, 1980:60).

GUIDE HILL 82°45′N 64°30′W, rising to c. 320 m near the head of James Ross Bay, was charted by the BAE in April 1876 and so named as a reference point (BA chart 275, 1877; BPP, 1877, chart facing p. 126; DMR sheet 29^{A}N½, 19^{A}N½ and 9^{A}N½, 1944; CBGN, 1960; DEMR sheet 120 F & 120 G, 1967; CPCGN, 1980:70).

GULL GLACIER 81°24′N 77°25′W, forms an ice tongue flowing ESE towards the NW shore of Tanquary Fiord; following field work from the DRB Tanquary Camp in 1962–63, was so named because a glaucous gull (*Larus hyperboreus*) was observed in the vicinity in May 1962 (CPCGN Decisions, 1963; DEMR sheet 340 D, 1967; CPCGN, 1980:70).

GYPSUM RIVER 82°41′N 68°10′W, on Arthur Laing Peninsula, flows SE, E, and S to the NW shore of Clements Markham Inlet; following field work from the DRB Gilman Glacier camp in 1957–58, was so named from the occurrence of gypsum in Permo-Carboniferous beds in the locality (CBGN, 1960; Christie, 1962, Map 20; DEMR sheet 120 F & 120 G, 1967; CPCGN, 1980:70).

HALL BASIN 81°30′N 63°00′W, sea area bounded to the N and S by Robeson Channel and Kennedy Channel, and to the E and W by the Greenland coast and Lady Franklin Bay, was roughly charted by Hayes in May 1861 (Hayes, 1867, chart facing p. 72); further charted by the USNPE in August 1871 and by the BAE in August 1875; named by the USNPE after Captain Charles Francis Hall (1821–71), American Arctic explorer, Commander of two Franklin search

expeditions, 1860–62 and 1864–69, and of the USNPE until his death in North Greenland (BA chart 275, 1875; Ravenstein, 1875, map; BPP, 1877, chart facing p. 38; GBC, 1910, map; DMR sheet 29^{A}s½, 19^{A}s½ and 9^{A}s½, 1944; DEMR sheet 120 C & 120 D, 1967; CPCGN, 1980:71).

HAMILTON BLUFF 82°50′N 65°35′W, line of cliffs at the W entrance of Parker Bay, Clements Markham Inlet, was charted by the BAE in April 1876 and named probably after Admiral Sir Richard Vesey Hamilton (1829–1912), member of Franklin search expeditions, 1850–51 and 1852–54, First Sea Lord of the Admiralty, 1889–91, and President, Royal Naval College Greenwich, 1891–94, ([referring to the W entrance point of Parker Bay] BA chart 275, 1877; BPP,1877, chart facing p. 172; [referring to cliffs on SE side of Clements Markham Inlet] DMR sheet 29^{A}N½, 19^{A}N½ and 9^{A}N½, 1944; [as now defined] CBGN, 1960; DEMR sheet 120 F & 120 G, 1967; CPCGN, 1980:71). *Beverley Point*, also referring to the W entrance point of Parker Bay after C.J. Beverley (*Mount Beverley*, q.v.) (BPP, 1877, chart facing p. 172).

Hamilton Fish, Cape: see Hamilton Fish Peak.

HAMILTON FISH PEAK 82°48′N 63°30′W, rising steeply to c. 245 m above the E shore of Feilden Peninsula, was sighted by the USNPE in September 1871 (Davis, 1876:85) and called *Cape Hamilton Fish* after Hamilton Fish (1808–93), U.S. Secretary of State, 1869–77, and one of the negotiators of the Treaty of Washington in May 1871 (BA chart 275, 1875; Ravenstein, map, 1875);

charted by the BAE in September 1875 and named *Hamilton Fish Peak* (BPP, 1877, chart facing p. 172; DMR sheet 29^AN½, 19^AN½ and 9^AN½, 1944; CBGN, 1960; DEMR sheet 120 E, 1966; CPCGN, 1980:71).

HARE POINT 81°27′N 67°05′W, on the NW side of Archer Fiord, S of Mount Grinnell, was charted by the BAE in April 1876 and named after the arctic hare (*Lepus arcticus*), seen in numbers at this point (BA chart 275, 1877; BPP, 1877, chart facing p. 38; CPCGN Decisions, 1969; CPCGN, 1980:72; DEMR sheet 120 C & 120 D, 1986).

HARLEY RIDGE 82°30′N 75°30′W, runs N-S and rises to c. 1580 m on the E side of M'Clintock Glacier; following field work by the GSC in 1980, was named after Petty Officer Daniel W. Harley, RN, Captain of the Foretop in HMS *Alert*, a member of the BAE northern sledge party which reached 83°20′N (CPCGN Decisions, 1982; DEMR sheet 340 E & 340 H, 1986).

Harley Spit: see Belknap, Cape.

HAZEN CAMP 81°48′N 71°01′W, on the NW shore of *Lake Hazen* (q.v.), NW of Johns Island, was established in April 1957 as a Canadian station for the IGY, 1957–58 (Hattersley-Smith, 1974:39–51); so named in association with the lake (CBGN, 1960; DEMR sheet 120 C & 120 D, 1967; CPCGN, 1980:2); has been used as a field station since the IGY and, since 1986, has been maintained by Parks Canada.

HAZEN, LAKE 81°50′N 70°25′W, the largest lake in the world N of 80° N,

extends 76 km ENE-WSW from the Turnabout River to the Very River, with a maximum width of 12 km and is drained by the Ruggles River from the SE shore; was discovered by the LFBE, 30 April 1882, and mapped in May and June of that year; named after Major General William Babcock Hazen (1830–87), Chief Signal Officer, U.S. Army, 1880–87, with responsibility for organizing the LFBE and under whose orders the expedition operated (BA chart 275, 1885; Greely, 1886, Vol. 1:272 and map p. 390; GBC, 1910:378; DMR sheets 29^AS½, 19^AS½ and 9^AS½, 49^AS½ and 39^AS½, 1944; CBGN, 1957; DEMR sheets 120 C & 120 D, 340 D, 1967; CPCGN, 1980:74). *Hazen Lake* (GBC, 1910, map).

Hazen Lake: see Hazen, Lake.

HECLA, CAPE 82°54′N 64°52′W, N point of *Parry Peninsula* (q.v.), was charted by the BAE in April 1876 and named after HMS *Hecla*, Parry's ship on his Arctic expeditions of 1819–20, 1821–23, and 1824–25 (BA chart 275, 1877; BPP, 1877, chart facing p. 126; GBC, 1910, map; DMR sheet 29^AN½, 19^AN½ and 9^AN½, 1944; DEMR sheet 120 F & 120 G, 1967; CPCGN, 1980:74); also called *Cape Parry* after Sir W.E. Parry (BPP, 1877, chart facing p. 172).

HEINTZELMAN LAKE 81°42′N 66°56′W, in Black Rock Vale W of Discovery Harbour, was roughly mapped by the LFBE in June 1882 and named *Lake Heintzelman*, probably after Major General Samuel Peter Heintzelman (1805–80), of the U.S. Army (Greely, 1886, Vol. 1: 366). *Heintzelman Lake* (Greely, 1886, Vol. 1, map p. 390; DMR sheet 29^AS½, 19^AS½ and 9^AS½, 1944; CBGN, 1960; DEMR sheet 120 C & 120 D, 1967; CPCGN, 1980:74).

Heintzelman, Lake: see Heintzelman Lake.

HENRIETTA NESMITH GLACIER
81°50′N 73°00′W, flowing SE almost to the NW shore of Lake Hazen, was roughly mapped by the LFBE in May 1882 and named after Henrietta H.C. Nesmith (Mrs. A.W. Greely), wife of the Commander of the expedition (BA chart 275, 1885; Greely, 1886, Vol. 1:282–88 and map p. 390; DMR sheet 49^{A}S½ and 39^{A}S½, 1944; CBGN, 1960; Christie, 1962, Map 20; DEMR sheet 340 D, 1967; CPCGN, 1980:75).

HENRIETTA RIVER 81°44′N 72°25′W, drains Henrietta Nesmith Glacier and flows SE in a braided channel into Lake Hazen; following field work from the DRB Hazen Camp in 1957–58, was so named in association with the glacier (CBGN, 1960; DEMR sheet 340 D, 1967; CPCGN, 1980:75).

HILGARD BAY 82°27′N 63°15′W, the inner part of *Black Cliffs Bay* (q.v.). The name was originally applied to the whole bay by the USNPE in September 1871 after Julius Erasmus Hilgard (1825–91), American physicist and Superintendent, U.S. Coast Survey (BA chart 275, 1875; Ravenstein, map, 1875; BPP, 1877, chart facing p. 172; GBC, 1910:380; [as now defined] DMR sheet 29^{A}N½, 19^{A}N½ and 9^{A}N½, 1944; CBGN, 1953; DEMR sheet 120 E, 1966; CPCGN, 1980:76).

Hilgard Bay: see Black Cliffs Bay.

HILGARD CREEK 82°27′N 63°12′W, flowing NW from Hilgard Lake to the

SE shore of *Hilgard Bay* (q.v.), was so named in association with the bay (CPCGN Decisions, 1962; CPCGN, 1980:76; DEMR sheet 120 E, 1988).

HILGARD LAKE 82°26′N, 63°09′W on the SE side of *Hilgard Bay* (q.v.), following field work in the area by the Geographical Branch, DMTS, in 1958, was so named in association with the bay (CBGN, 1959; CPCGN, 1980:76; DEMR sheet 120 E, 1988).

HILGARD, MOUNT 82°22′N 63°40′W, rises to c. 620 m SW of *Hilgard Bay* (q.v.); following field work in the area by the Geographical Branch, DMTS, in 1952, was so named in association with the bay (CBGN, 1959; DEMR sheet 120 E, 1966; CPCGN, 1980:76).

HILGARD RIVER 82°27′N 63°28′W, flows N and E into *Hilgard Bay* (q.v.); following field work by the Geographical Branch, DMTS, in 1952, was so named in association with the bay (CBGN, 1953; DEMR sheet 120 E, 1966; CPCGN, 1980:76).

Hog Back: see Hogback Mountain.

HOGBACK MOUNTAIN 81°49′N 64°47′W, rising to c. 790 m N of Fort Conger, was roughly charted by the BAE and named *Hog Back* from the gently curving outline of its summit (BA chart 275, 1877; BPP, 1877, chart facing p. 62; Greely, 1886, Vol. 1, map facing p. 87; DMR sheet 29^{A}S½, 19^{A}S½ and 9^{A}S½, 1944). *The Hogback* (Greely, 1886, Vol. 1:91). *Hogback Mountain* (GBC, 1910:380; CPCGN Decisions, 1969; CPCGN, 1980:76; DEMR sheet 120 C & 120 D, 1986).

Hogback, The: see Hogback Mountain.

HOLLINS CREEK 82°28'N 63°06'W, flows N into Hilgard Bay; following field work in the area by the Geographical Branch, DMTS, in 1952, was named after Private John Hollins, RMLI, of HMS *Alert* (CBGN, 1953; DEMR sheet 120 E, 1966; CPCGN, 1980:76).

HORNBY, MOUNT 82°59'N 70°30'W, rising to c. 950 m on Arthur Laing Peninsula, E of Markham Fiord, was roughly charted by the BAE in April 1876 and named after Admiral of the Fleet Sir (Geoffrey Thomas) Phipps Hornby (1825–95), Commander-in-Chief, Mediterranean, 1877–80, and Portsmouth, 1882–85 (BA chart 275, 1877; BPP, 1877, chart facing p. 172; GBC, 1910:382; DMR sheet 29ᴬN½, 19ᴬN½ and 9ᴬN½, 1944; DEMR sheet 120 F & 120 G, 1967; CPCGN, 1980:78).

IDA BAY 81°31'N 68°35'W, forming the WSW extremity of Conybeare Fiord, was mapped by the LFBE in April 1882 and so named (BA chart 275, 1885; Greely, 1886, Vol. 1:268 and map p. 390; DMR sheet 29ᴬs½, 19ᴬs½ and 9ᴬs½, 1944; CBGN, 1960; DEMR sheet 120 C & 120 D, 1967; CPCGN, 1980:80).

IDA RIVER 81°33'N 68°54'W, flows E into the head of *Ida Bay* (q.v.); following field work from the DRB Hazen Camp in 1957–58, was so named in association with the bay (CBGN, 1960; DEMR sheet 120 C & 120 D, 1967; CPCGN, 1980:80).

ÎLE-D'ELLESMERE, RÉSERVE DE PARC NATIONAL DE L' 82°13'N 72°13'W: see Ellesmere Island National Park Reserve.

JAEGER CREEK 81°30'N 68°59'W, flows SE into the head of Ida Bay, Conybeare Fiord; following field work by the PCSP in 1971, was so named in reference to a long-tailed jaeger (*Stercorarius longicaudus*) seen there (CPCGN Decisions, 1977; CPCGN, 1980:84; DEMR sheet 120 C & 120 D, 1986).

JAMES ROSS BAY 82°50'N 64°25'W, between Parry Peninsula and Feilden Peninsula, with entrance points at Cape Hecla and Cape Joseph Henry, was charted by the BAE in April 1876 and named after Rear Admiral Sir James Clark Ross (1800–62), member of his uncle (Sir) John Ross's 1818 Arctic expedition, member of Parry's Arctic expeditions, 1819–20, 1821–1823, 1824–25, and 1827, of John Ross's Arctic expedition, 1829–33 (discovering the North Magnetic Pole in 1831), and Commander of the Antarctic expedition, 1839–43, in HMS *Erebus (Crozier Island*, q.v.) and of the Franklin search expedition, 1848–49 (BA chart 275, 1877; BPP, 1877, chart facing p. 126; GBC, 1910, map; DMR sheet 29ᴬN½, 19ᴬN½ and 9ᴬN½, 1944; DEMR sheet 120 F & 120 G, 1967; CPCGN, 1980:85).

JAMES ROSS RIVER 82°48'N 64°40'W, flows NE and N from the United States Range into the W side of *James Ross Bay* (q.v.); following field work by a DRB-GSC party in 1953, was so named in association with the bay (CBGN, 1960; DEMR sheet 120 F & 120 G, 1967; CPCGN, 1980:85).

JOHNS ISLAND 81°49'N 71°04'W, off the NW shore of Lake Hazen near Hazen Camp, was roughly mapped by the LFBE in April 1882 and named

John's Island (Greely, 1886, Vol. 1:277 and map p. 390). *Johns Island* (BA chart 275, 1885; DMR sheet 29ᴬs½, 19ᴬs½ and 9ᴬs½, 1944; CBGN, 1960; DEMR sheet 120 c & 120 d, 1967; CPCGN, 1980:86).

John's Island: see Johns Island.

JOINER CREEK 82°32′N 63°08′W, flows ENE into Knot Bay, Black Cliffs Bay; following field work in the area by the Geographical Branch, DMTS, in 1952, was named after Leading Stoker Robert Joiner, RN, of HMS *Alert* (CBGN, 1953; DEMR sheet 120 e, 1966; CPCGN, 1980:86).

JOLLIFFE BAY 82°31′N 62°40′W, S of Williams Island, Black Cliffs Bay, was charted by the BAE in September 1875 and named after Petty Officer Thomas Jolliffe, RN, Captain of Maintop in HMS *Alert* (BPP, 1877, chart facing p. 88; CBGN, 1959; CPCGN, 1980:86; DEMR sheet 120 e, 1988).

JOLLIFFE, CAPE 82°31′N 62°47′W, between Colan Bay and *Jolliffe Bay* (q.v.), was charted by the BAE in September 1875 (BPP, 1877, chart facing p. 172); following field work by the Geographical Branch, DMTS, in 1958, so named in association with the bay (CBGN, 1959; DEMR sheet 120 e, 1966; CPCGN, 1980:86).

JOSEPH HENRY, CAPE 82°49′N 63°30′W, NE point of Feilden Peninsula, was sighted by the USNPE in September 1871 (Davis, 1876:85 and map between p. 356–57); named by the USNPE after Joseph Henry (1797–1878), American physicist, Professor of Natural Philosophy at College of New Jersey (later Princeton University),

1832–46, and later first Director of the Smithsonian Institution (BA chart 275, 1875; Ravenstein, 1975, map; BPP, 1877, chart facing p. 78; GBC, 1910:384 and map; DMR sheet 29ᴬN½, 19ᴬN½ and 9ᴬN½, 1944; DEMR sheet 120 e, 1966; CPCGN, 1980:86).

Judge Daly Peninsula: see Judge Daly Promontory.

JUDGE DALY PROMONTORY 81°15′N 67°00′W, between Archer Fiord and Kennedy Channel, extending SW from Cape Baird to a line joining the head of Ella Bay and Carl Ritter Bay, was roughly charted on its SE coast by Hayes in May 1861 and by the USNPE in August 1871 (Hayes 1867, chart facing p. 72; Ravenstein, 1875, map); further charted by the BAE in August 1875 and April 1876, and named *Judge Daly Peninsula* after Charles Patrick Daly (1816–99), New York judge, 1844–86, and President of the American Geographical Society from 1864 (Nares, 1878, Vol. 1:334; GBC Decisions, 1910). *Judge Daly Promontory* (BA chart 275, 1877; DMR sheet 29ᴬs½, 19ᴬs½ and 9ᴬs½, 1944; DEMR sheet 120 c & 120 d, 1967; CPCGN, 1980:87).

JULIA, MOUNT 82°45′N 64°10′W, rising to c. 620 m on Feilden Peninsula, was sighted by the USNPE in September 1871 (Davis, 1876:85); so named by the USNPE, and charted by the BAE in April 1876 (BA chart 275, 1875; Ravenstein, 1875, map; BPP, 1877, chart facing p. 126; DMR sheet 29ᴬN½, 19ᴬN½ and 9ᴬN½, 1944; CBGN, 1960; DEMR sheet 120 f & 120 g, 1967; CPCGN, 1980:87).

KENNEDY CHANNEL 80°55'N 66°30'W, running NNE-SSW from Hall Basin to Kane Basin and separating eastern Ellesmere Island from North Greenland, was roughly charted throughout its length by Kane in 1854 and named after Captain William Kennedy, British master mariner, who commanded *Prince Albert* on a Franklin search expedition to the Barrow Strait area, 1850–51; further charted by the USNPE in September 1871 and by the BAE in September 1875 (Kane, 1856, Vol. 1, chart facing p. 5, p. 290; Hayes, 1867, chart facing p. 72; BA chart 275, 1875; Ravenstein, 1875, map; BPP, 1877, chart facing p. 38; GBC, 1910, end map; DMR sheet 29ᴬs½, 19ᴬs½ and 9ᴬs½, 1944; DEMR sheet 120 C & 120 D, 1967; CPCGN, 1980:89).

KENNEDY, MOUNT 81°08'N 77°35'W, rising to c. 1200 m and forming the S summit of the ice cap E of Cape Gleason, Tanquary Fiord, was roughly mapped by the CLE in May 1915 and named after L.E. Kennedy, American geologist of the University of Illinois (GBC Decisions, 1928; DMR sheet 49ᴬs½ and 39ᴬs½, 1944; CPCGN, 1980:89).

KENSINGTON LAKE 81°45'N 72°54'W, on the SW side of the terminus of Henrietta Nesmith Glacier and drained by the *Kensington River* (q.v.), following field work from the DRB Hazen Camp in 1957–58, was so named in association with the river (CPCGN Decisions, 1968; CPCGN, 1980:89; DEMR sheet 340 D, 1988).

KENSINGTON RIVER 81°46'N 72°42'W, flows ENE from Turnstone Glacier to Henrietta Nesmith Glacier,

then joins the Henrietta River to flow SE into Lake Hazen; following field work from the DRB Hazen Camp in 1957–58, was so named in reference to Kensington Gardens, London, because of the relatively lush vegetation in the river valley (CPCGN Decisions, 1968; CPCGN, 1980:89; DEMR sheet 340 D, 1988).

KEPPEL HEAD 81°31'N 66°37'W, W entrance point of Archer Fiord, Lady Franklin Bay, was charted by the BAE in April 1876 and named *Keppel's Head*, after Admiral of the Fleet Sir Henry Keppel (1809–1904), Commander-in-Chief, Devonport, 1872–75 (BPP, 1877, chart facing p. 336) or *Keppel Head* (BA chart 275, 1877; BPP, 1877, chart facing p. 38; DMR sheet 29ᴬs½, 19ᴬs½ and 9ᴬs½, 1944; DEMR sheet 120 C & 120 D, 1967; CPCGN, 1980:89).

Keppel's Head: see Keppel Head.

KETTLE LAKE 81°24'N 76°43'W, on a kame terrace SE of Tanquary Camp, following field work from the DRB camp, 1962–68, was so named because the feature is a true "kettle" lake in the glacio-morphological sense (CPCGN Decisions, 1971; CPCGN, 1980:90; DEMR sheet 340 D, 1988).

KILBOURNE LAKE 81°52'N 68°25'W, between the head of Black Rock Vale and Craig Lake, was roughly mapped by the LFBE in June 1882 and named *Lake Kilbourne,* probably after Major Charles Evans Kilbourne (1844–1903), who served in the U.S. Army Signal Service, 1871–84 and 1890–93 (Greely, 1886, Vol. 1:374). *Kilbourne Lake* (CBGN, 1960; DEMR sheet 120 C & 120 D, 1967; CPCGN, 1980:90).

Kilbourne, Lake: see Kilbourne Lake.

KIRK CREEK 82°28′N 62°49′W, flows
N from Winchester Hills into Colan
Bay, draining *Kirk Lake* (q.v.);
following field work by the
Geographical Branch, DMTS, in 1952,
was so named in association with the
lake (CBGN, 1953; DEMR sheet 120 E,
1966; CPCGN, 1980:91).

KIRK LAKE 82°28′N 62°49′W, on
Smith Peninsula S of the head of
Colan Bay, following field work by
the Geographical Branch, DMTS, in
1952, was named after Dr. D.W. Kirk
(d. 1950), Canadian geographer, who
was killed in the crash of an RCAF
Lancaster aircraft (Wing Commander
D. French, RCAF) at Alert, 31 July 1950
(CBGN, 1953; DEMR sheet 120 E, 1966;
CPCGN, 1980:91).

KNOT BAY 82°33′N 63°05′W, W side of
Black Cliffs Bay at the mouth of
Joiner Creek, was charted by the BAE
in May 1876 and called *Knots Harbour*
(BPP, 1877, chart facing p. 126) or *Knot
Harbour* (BA chart 275, 1877; Nares
1878, Vol. 1:329; GBC, 1910:390; DMR
sheet 29^{A}N½, 19^{A}N½ and 9^{A}N½,
1944), after a number of knot (*Calidris
canutus*) observed there. *Knot Bay*
(CBGN, 1953; DEMR sheet 120 E, 1966;
CPCGN, 1980:92).

Knot(s) Harbour: see Knot Bay.

KOCH, MOUNT 81°11′N 75°20′W,
rising to c. 1050 m S of the head of
the Macdonald River, was roughly
mapped by the CLE in May 1915 and
named after Dr. (Svend) Lauge Koch
(1892–1964), Greenland explorer and
State Geologist, Geological Survey of

Greenland; member of Second Thule
Expedition to North Greenland,
1916–18, and leader of Greenland
expeditions, 1920–58 (GBC Decisions,
1928; DMR sheet 49^{A}s½ and 39^{A}s½,
1944; CPCGN, 1980:92; DEMR sheet
340 D, 1988).

LADY FRANKLIN BAY 81°35′N
64°30′W, between Distant Cape and
Cape Baird, leads N into Discovery
Harbour, W into Conybeare Fiord,
and SW into Archer Fiord; was sighted
by Kane in June 1854 and named after
Jane, Lady Franklin (1792–1875),
second wife of Captain Sir John
Franklin (1786–1847), Arctic explorer
(she was the foremost promoter of the
Franklin search expeditions); sighted
by Hayes in May 1861, and charted by
the USNPE in August 1871 and by the
BAE in September 1875 (Kane, 1856,
Vol. 1, chart facing p. 5; Hayes, 1867,
chart facing p. 72, p. 374; GBC,
1910:392 and map; DMR sheet 29^{A}s½,
19^{A}s½ and 9^{A}s½, 1944; DEMR sheet
120 C & 120 D, 1967; CPCGN,
1980:94). *Lady Franklin Strait*
(Ravenstein, 1875, map; BPP, 1877,
chart facing p. 1). *Lady Franklin Sound*
(BA chart 275, 1877; BPP 1877, chart
facing p. 38; Nares, 1878, Vol. 2:84).

Lady Franklin Sound, Strait: see Lady
Franklin Bay.

Lawrence Bay: see Dana Bay.

LEWIS LAKE 81°30′N 74°35′W, in the
valley of the *Lewis River* (q.v.),
following field work from the DRB
Hazen Camp in 1957–58, was so
named in association with the river
(CPCGN Decisions, 1968; CPCGN,
1980:97; DEMR sheet 340 D, 1988).

LEWIS RIVER 81°30′N 74°26′W, flowing SE from the Scylla and Charybdis Glaciers to join the Very River, was roughly mapped by the LFBE in July 1882 and named *W.H. Lewis River* (Greely, 1886, Vol. 1:404). *Lewis River* (Greely, 1886, Vol. 2:437; DMR sheet 49^{A}s½ and 39^{A}s½, 1944; CBGN, 1960; Christie, 1962, Map 20; DEMR sheet 340 D, 1967; CPCGN, 1980:97).

LIEBER, CAPE 81°29′N 64°26′W, S of Cape Baird, Kennedy Channel, was roughly charted by Hayes in May 1861 and named after Dr. Francis Lieber (1798–1872), German-born American political philosopher and Professor of History and Political Economy, Columbia College (now Columbia University), New York, 1856–72 (Hayes, 1867, chart facing p. 72, p. 374); further charted by the USNPE in August 1871 and by the BAE in August 1875; (BA chart 275, 1875; Ravenstein, 1875, map; BAE, 1877, chart facing p. 38; GBC Decisions, 1910; DMR sheet 29^{A}s½, 19^{A}s½ and 9^{A}s½, 1944; DEMR sheet 120 C & 120 D, 1967; CPCGN, 1980:97).

LINCOLN BAY 82°07′N 61°50′W, SW of Cape Union, Robeson Channel, with Cape Frederick VII as its SW entrance point, was charted by the USNPE in August 1871 (Davis, 1876:85); named by the USNPE after Abraham Lincoln (1809–65), 16th President of the United States, 1860–65 (BA chart 275, 1875; Ravenstein, 1875, map; BPP, 1877, chart facing p. 116; DMR sheet 29^{A}N½, 19^{A}N½ and 9^{A}N½, 1944; CBGN, 1960; DEMR sheet 120 E, 1966; CPCGN, 1980:98).

LINCOLN, MER DE 62°00′N 82°30′W: see Lincoln Sea.

LINCOLN SEA/LINCOLN, MER DE 62°00′N 82°30′W, sea area N of Robeson Channel and roughly between Cape Joseph Henry and John Murray Ø, North Greenland, was reached by the USNPE in September 1871 (Davis, 1876:85); named by the USNPE after Abraham Lincoln (*Lincoln Bay,* q.v.) and charted along its coastline by the BAE (BA chart 275, 1875; Ravenstein, 1875, map; Davis, 1876, map between p. 356 and 357; DMR sheet 29^{A}N½, 19^{A}N½ and 9^{A}N½, 1944; CBGN, 1953; DEMR sheet 120 E, 1966; CPCGN, 1980:98).

LONESOME CREEK 81°33′N 66°59′W, flows NE into Conybeare Fiord, NW of Keppel Head; following field work by the GSC from the DRB Hazen Camp in 1957–58, was so named after a Greenland dog of that name (CBGN, 1960; DEMR sheet 120 C & 120 D, 1967; CPCGN, 1980:99).

LORIMER RIDGE 82°35′N 72°12′W, rises to c. 1070 m on the E side of Disraeli Glacier; following field work by the GSC in 1979, was named after Able Seaman William Lorimer, RN, of HMS *Alert,* a member of a BAE sledge party in support of the western journey (CPCGN Decisions, 1980; DEMR sheet 340 E & 340 H, 1986; sheet 120 F & 120 G, 1987).

LOWER DUMBELL LAKE 82°30′N 62°37′W, W of Alert and the western of two lakes supplying water to the station, was charted by the BAE in September 1875 and, with *Upper Dumbell Lake* (q.v.), included under the name *Dumb Bell Lakes* from the disposition of the two lakes in plan (BA chart 275, 1877; BPP, 1877, chart facing p. 126; DMR sheet 29ᴬN½, 19ᴬN½ and 9ᴬN½, 1944); following field work by the Geographical Branch, DMTS, in 1952, named *Lower Dumbell Lake* (CBGN, 1953; DEMR sheet 120 E, 1966; CPCGN, 1980:101).

LYNN, MOUNT 81°23′N 74°46′W, rising to c. 1250 m E of the head of the Very River, was roughly mapped by the LFBE in July 1882 and named after Sergeant David Lynn (d. 1884), of the Second Cavalry, U.S. Army, a member of the sledge party at the time (Greely, 1886, Vol. 1, map p. 390, p. 402; DMR sheet 49ᴬs½ and 39ᴬs½, 1944; CPCGN Decisions, 1968; CPCGN, 1980:101; DEMR sheet 340 D, 1988). *Lynn Mountain* (GBC, 1910:398).

Lynn Mountain: see Lynn, Mount.

M'Clintock Bay: see M'Clintock Inlet.

M'CLINTOCK GLACIER 82°19′N 75°40′W, flows N from the main ice cap of northern Ellesmere Island into the head of *M'Clintock Inlet* (q.v.); following field work from the DRB Gilman Glacier camp in 1957−58, was so named in association with the inlet (CBGN, 1960; Christie, 1962, Map 20; DEMR sheet 340 E & 340 H, 1967; CPCGN, 1980:108).

M'Clintock Ice Shelf 82°55′N 77°30′W, formerly occupying the outer part of *M'Clintock Inlet* (q.v.), was so named in association with the inlet (CBGN, 1960; DEMR sheet 340 E and 340 H, 1967; CPCGN, 1980:108). Following the almost complete disintegration of the ice shelf by July 1966 (Hattersley-Smith, 1967), the name was rescinded (CPCGN Decisions, 1984).

M'CLINTOCK INLET 82°45′N 76°30′W, extends SE from its entrance between Bromley Peak and Cape Discovery; was charted in its outer part by the BAE in May 1876, when the name *M'Clintock Bay* was applied to the entire feature between Cape Richards and Cape Discovery, after Admiral Sir (Francis) Leopold M'Clintock (1819−1907), Arctic explorer, member of Franklin search expeditions 1848−49, 1850−51, and 1852−54, and Commander of the search expedition in SY *Fox*, which found Franklin records; Admiral Superintendent, Portsmouth Dockyard, 1872−77, and Commander-in-Chief, North American and West Indian Station, 1879−82 (BA chart 275, 1877; BPP, 1877, chart facing p. 172, p. 204; GBC, 1910:398−99; DMR sheet 49ᴬN½ and 39ᴬN½, 1944). *M'Clintock Inlet*, as now defined (Christie, 1962, Map 20; DEMR sheet 340 E & 340 H, 1967; CPCGN, 1980:108).

MACDONALD RIVER 81°25′N 76°55′W, flows NW into the head of Tanquary Fiord just NE of Tanquary Camp; following field work from the DRB camp in 1962−63, was named after the icebreaker CCGS *John A. Macdonald* (Captain P.M. Fournier) which, in August 1962, performed the sealift for the establishment of the camp, becoming the first ship to penetrate the fiord on the most northerly voyage (at that time) of a Canadian ship, and relieving the camp in subsequent years (CPCGN Decisions, 1965; DEMR sheet 340 D, 1967; CPCGN, 1980:102).

McGILL MOUNTAIN 81°50′N 71°35′W, rises to c. 1085 m NW of Hazen Camp; was named after McGill University, Montreal, four graduate students of which manned the DRB camp during the 1957–58 winter and formed part of the 1958 summer party (CBGN, 1960; DEMR sheet 120 C & 120 D, 1967; CPCGN, 1980:107).

McKINLEY BAY 81°08′N 79°12′W, between Cape Macoun and Cape Fernald, Tanquary Fiord, extending NW to Chapman Glacier, was roughly mapped by the CLE in May 1915 and named after William Brown McKinley (1856–1926), Member of the U.S. Congress for the Illinois District, 1905–13 and 1915–21, and U.S. Senator, 1921–27 (GBC Decisions, 1928; DMR sheet 49^{As}½ and 39^{As}½, 1944; DEMR sheet 340 D, 1967; CPCGN Decisions, 1968; CPCGN, 1980:107).

MACOUN, CAPE 81°05′N 79°03′W, SW entrance point of McKinley Bay, Tanquary Fiord, was roughly mapped by the CLE in May 1915 and named after John Macoun (1831–1920), Canadian field naturalist; Dominion Botanist, 1882–1912, and Deputy Director, GSC, 1887–1912, whose collections of fauna and flora became the foundation for the National Museum of Natural Sciences, Ottawa (GBC Decisions, 1928; DMR sheet 49^{As}½ and 39^{As}½, 1944; DEMR sheet 340 D, 1967; CPCGN, 1980:102).

MANN BAY 82°29′N 61°38′W, SE of Mann Point, was charted by the BAE in September 1875 (BPP, 1877, chart facing p. 126); following field work by the Geographical Branch, DMTS, in 1952, was named after Shipwright Henry Mann, RN, of HMS *Alert* (CBGN,

1953; CPCGN, 1980:104; DEMR sheet 120 E, 1987).

MANN POINT 82°29′N 61°39′W, between Mushroom Point and Cape Sheridan, forming the NW entrance point of *Mann Bay* (q.v.), was so named in association with the bay (CPCGN Decisions, 1962; DEMR sheet 120 E, 1966; CPCGN, 1980:104).

MANN RIVER 82°29′N 61°39′W, flows NE into *Mann Bay* (q.v.); following field work by the Geographical Branch, DMTS, in 1952, was so named in association with the bay (CBGN, 1952; CPCGN, 1980:104; DEMR sheet 120 E, 1987).

Marco Polo Bay: see Patterson Bay.

MARINE GLACIER 82°17′N 78°45′W, flows E into the head of Milne Glacier; following mountaineering in the area by the RNEIE, whose main camp was established here in 1972, was so named in association with three Royal Marines on that expedition and with the original Royal Naval explorers of the N coast of Ellesmere Island (CPCGN Decisions, 1973; CPCGN, 1980:105; DEMR sheet 340 E & 340 H, 1988).

Markham Bay: see Markham Fiord.

MARKHAM FIORD 82°59′N 71°20′W, on the E side of Cranstone Peninsula, extending S and SE from its W entrance point at Cape Nares, was charted in its outer part by the BAE in May 1876 and named *Markham Bay*, after Commander Albert Hastings (later Admiral Sir Albert) Markham, RN (1841–1918), Second-in-Command of HMS *Alert* and Leader of the northern sledge party; Commander-in-Chief at The Nore, 1901–04 (BA chart 275, 1877; BPP, 1877, chart facing p. 172; GBC, 1910:403 and map; DMR sheet 29^{A}N½, 19^{A}N½ and 9^{A}N½, 1944). *Markham Fiord* (DEMR sheet 120 F & 120 G, 1967; CPCGN, 1980:105).

Markham Inlet: see Clements Markham Inlet.

MARVIN ISLANDS 82°59′N 73°37′W, in the entrance of Disraeli Fiord, following field work by the DRB-GSC-AFCRC group in 1954, were named after Professor Ross G. Marvin (1874–1909), of the Columbia College of Civil Engineering, a member of Peary's North Pole expedition, 1908–09, who was drowned while returning to Cape Columbia from 86°38′N, in command of one of Peary's supporting parties (CBGN, 1960; Christie, 1962, Map 20; DEMR sheet 340 E & 340 H, 1967; CPCGN, 1980:105).

MARVIN PENINSULA 82°50′N 75°00′W, between M'Clintock Inlet and Disraeli Fiord, following field work by the GSC in 1965, was named after Ross G. Marvin (*Marvin Islands,* q.v.) (CPCGN Decisions, 1966; DEMR sheet 340 E & 340 H, 1967; CPCGN, 1980:105).

MARY PEAK 82°46′N 64°05′W, rising to c. 670 m on Feilden Peninsula, was sighted by the USNPE in September 1871 (Davis, 1876:85); so named by the USNPE and charted by the BAE in April 1876 (BA chart 275, 1875; Ravenstein, 1875, map; BPP, 1877, chart facing p. 126; DMR sheet 29^{A}N½, 19^{A}N½ and 9^{A}N½, 1944; DEMR sheet 120 F & 120 G, 1967; CPCGN, 1980:105).

MASKELL INLET 82°52′N 78°30′W, W arm of an unnamed fiord S of Bromley Peak, following field work by the GSC in 1979, was named after Able Seaman William Maskell, RN (1853–1942), of HMS *Alert* on the BAE and a member of the northern sledge party (CPCGN, 1980; DEMR sheet 340 E & 340 H, 1988).

MAY CREEK 81°24′N 76°55′W, flows NW into Tanquary Fiord and provides fresh water at Tanquary Camp, where it is dammed to form a small pond; following field work from the camp from 1962, was so named because it starts to flow in late May (CPCGN Decisions, 1971; CPCGN, 1980:6; DEMR sheet 340 D, 1988).

MAY CREEK 82°30′N 62°37′W, flows N from Winchester Hills into Lower Dumbell Lake; following field work by the Geographical Branch, DMTS, in 1952, was named after Lieutenant William Henry May, RN (1849–1930), junior lieutenant in HMS *Alert*; later Admiral of the Fleet Sir William May; Commander-in-Chief, Devonport, 1911–13 (CBGN, 1953; DEMR sheet 120 E, 1966; CPCGN, 1980:104).

MESA CREEK 81°54′N 69°47′W, flows SE into Lake Hazen SSW of the Gilman River; following field work from the DRB Hazen Camp in 1957–58, was so named from the landform in this locality (CBGN, 1960; DEMR sheet 120 C & 120 D, 1967; CPCGN, 1980:109).

MILLER ISLAND 81°34′N 66°35′W, off Lady Franklin Bay in the entrance to Conybeare Fiord, was charted by the BAE in April 1876 and named after Second Engineer Matthew Richard

Barbeau Peak (2616 m), the highest mountain in eastern North America, with the *British Empire Range* in the background.
Jerry Kobalenko/Parks Canada

Johns Island, basking in the 24-hour sunlight.
Wayne Lynch/Parks Canada

Looking south through the *Rollrock River* valley, one can see *Rollrock Lake*, which is blocked from drainage by *Rollrock Glacier*. Further along to the left is *Steeprock Glacier*, and in the distance is *Tanquary Fiord*.
Jerry Kobalenko/Parks Canada

Air Force Glacier.
Renee Wissink/Parks Canada

Gull Glacier at the head of *Tanquary Fiord.*
Renee Wissink/Parks Canada

The *Fort Conger* National Historic Site, located on the northeastern shore of *Discovery Harbour,*
seen looking towards *Mount Campbell* on *Bellot Island.*
Wayne Lynch/Parks Canada

Junction of the *Scylla* (left) and *Charybdis* (right) *Glaciers* as seen from *Mount Biederbick*, located along the *Lewis River* valley. Blocked by giant glaciers on either side sits *Ekblaw Lake*.
Parks Canada

August breakup of *Lake Hazen* as seen from *McGill Mountain*.
Steve Pinksen/Parks Canada

Herd of arctic hares in the upper *Snow Goose River* valley.
Renee Wissink/Parks Canada

Cairn at *Record Point* in *Archer Fiord*.
Renee Wissink/Parks Canada

Fiala Glacier at the head of the *Air Force River* valley.
Mike Beedell/Parks Canada

Looking northwest through *Bellows Valley*.
Barry Troke/Parks Canada

Omingmak Mountain on the north shore of *Lake Hazen.*
Brian Alexander/Parks Canada

Looking towards *Discovery Harbour* from the shore of *Heintzelman Lake.*
Renee Wissink/Parks Canada

The mountains of the *British Empire Range* pierce through the surrounding permanent icefields, up to 900 m thick and estimated to be more than 100,000 years old.
Wayne Lynch/Parks Canada

Walker Hill on *Ward Hunt Island*. Note the *Ward Hunt Ice Shelf* in the foreground.
Renee Wissink/Parks Canada

The head of *Clements Markham Inlet*, illustrating the raised marine silts in the foreground, with the
mountains of *Arthur Laing Peninsula* in the distance.
Parks Canada

Atop *Mount Timmia* looking at the *Redrock* (left) and *Cleaves* (right) *Glaciers.*
Jerry Kobalenko/Parks Canada

The *Ruggles River*, which usually flows year-round, is the only outlet for *Lake Hazen*.
The river drops about 158 m in elevation over its 29 km course.
Mike Cobus/Parks Canada

Mount Timmia.
Mike Beedell/Parks Canada

Blister Hill with *Lake Hazen* in the background.
Mike Cobus/Parks Canada

Tanquary Fiord.
Franco Barbagallo/Parks Canada

The *Henrietta Nesmith Glacier*, located at the southwest corner of *Lake Hazen*.
Wayne Lynch/Parks Canada

Steep calving wall of the *Henrietta Nesmith Glacier.*
Parks Canada

Two unnamed glaciers flowing down from the *Ad Astra Ice Cap*
to the floor of the *Air Force River* valley.
Parks Canada

The *Ward Hunt Ice Shelf.*
Franco Barbagallo/Parks Canada

The Peary Signpost as it stands today at *Cape Aldrich.*
Renee Wissink/Parks Canada

The *Scylla Glacier* spilling over from the *Viking Ice Cap*.
Wayne Lynch/Parks Canada

The *Roosevelt* Cairn, erected in 1906 by Ross Marvin, as it stands today overlooking *Floeberg Beach* on the edge of the *Arctic Ocean.*
Renee Wissink/Parks Canada

The *Ad Astra Ice Cap* viewed from the *Rollrock River* valley.
Wayne Lynch/Parks Canada

Miller, RN, of HMS *Discovery* (BA chart 275, 1877; BPP, 1877, chart facing p. 336; DMR sheet 29^{A}s½, 19^{A}s½ and 9^{A}s½, 1944; CBGN, 1960; DEMR sheet 120 C & 120 D, 1967; CPCGN, 1980:110).

MILNE GLACIER 82°24′N 80°00′W, flowing WNW into the head of Milne Fiord, was so named, in association with the fiord, after Admiral of the Fleet Sir Alexander Milne, 1st Baronet (1806–96), Junior Naval Lord of the Admiralty, 1866–68 and 1872–76, and Commander-in-Chief, Mediterranean, 1869–70 (CPCGN Decisions, 1968; CPCGN, 1980:110; DEMR sheet 340 E & 340 H, 1988).

MOSS BAY 82°57′N 67°16′W, SW of *Point Moss* (q.v.), Arthur Laing Peninsula, following field work by a DRB-GSC party in 1953, was so named in association with the point (CBGN, 1960; DEMR sheet 120 F & 120 G, 1967; CPCGN, 1980:113).

MOSS, POINT 82°58′N 67°09′W, E entrance point of Moss Bay, was charted by the BAE in April 1876 and named after Surgeon Edward Lawton Moss, MD, RN, Medical Officer and artist of HMS *Alert* (BA chart 275, 1877; BPP, 1877, chart facing p. 172, p. 191; GBC, 1910:407; DMR sheet 29^{A}N½, 19^{A}N½ and 9^{A}N½, 1944; DEMR sheet 120 F & 120 G, 1967; CPCGN, 1980:113).

MOSS POND 82°29′N 62°58′W, on Smith Peninsula E of Black Cliffs Bay, following field work by the Geographical Branch, DMTS, in 1952, was named after E.L. Moss of HMS *Alert* (*Point Moss,* q.v.) (CBGN, 1953; CPCGN, 1980:113; DEMR sheet 120 E, 1988).

MURCHISON, CAPE 81°46′N 64°06′W, SW entrance point of St. Patrick Bay, Robeson Channel, was sighted by Kane in June 1854 and named *Cape Roderick Murchison,* after Sir Roderick (Impey) Murchison, 1st Baronet (1792–1871), President of the Royal Geographical Society, 1843–45 and 1851–53, and Director General of the British Geological Survey from 1855 (Kane, 1856, Vol. 1, chart facing p. 5); sighted by Hayes in May 1861, but he applied the name *Mount Murchison* in error to a feature on Judge Daly Promontory (Hayes, 1867, chart facing p. 72); charted by the USNPE in August 1871, and by the BAE in September 1875 and April 1876. *Cape Murchison* (BA chart 275, 1875; BPP, 1877, chart facing p. 116; GBC, 1910:408; DMR sheet 29^{A}s½, 19^{A}s½ and 9^{A}s½, 1944; DEMR sheet 120 C & 120 D, 1967; CPCGN, 1980:114).

Murchison, Cape: see Distant Cape.

Murchison, Mount: see Murchison, Cape.

MURPHY POINT 82°52′N 77°00′W, on the W shore of M'Clintock Inlet, SE of Borup Point, following field work by the GSC in 1965, was named after John Murphy (b. 1875), Newfoundland Boatswain in ss *Roosevelt* of Peary's Arctic expeditions, 1905–06 and 1908–09 (CPCGN Decisions, 1966; DEMR sheet 340 E & 340 H, 1967; CPCGN, 1980:114).

MURRAY ICE CAP 81°21′N 69°24′W, rises to 1115 m E of *Murray Lake* (q.v.); following field work by the PCSP in 1977, was so named in association with the lake (CPCGN Decisions, 1978; CPCGN, 1980:114), but is not named on DEMR sheet 120 C & 120 D, 1988.

MURRAY ISLAND 81°15′N 69°19′W, in Simmons Bay on the NW side of Archer Fiord, was charted by the BAE in April 1876 and named after Private John Murray, RMLI, of HMS *Discovery* and a member of the sledge party to the fiord (BA chart 275, 1877; BPP, 1877, chart facing p. 336; CPCGN Decisions, 1969; CPCGN, 1980:114; DEMR sheet 120 C & 120 D, 1986).

MURRAY LAKE 81°20′N 69 19′W, mainly fills the valley running N from Simmons Bay, Archer Fiord; was roughly mapped by the LFBE in May 1883 (Greely, 1886, Vol. 2:39 and map facing p. 36); probably named later in association with *Murray Island* (q.v.) (DMR sheet 29ᴬs½, 19ᴬs½ and 9ᴬs½, 1944; CPCGN Decisions, 1969; CPCGN, 1980:114; DEMR sheet 120 C & 120 D, 1986).

MUSHROOM POINT 82°30′N 61°54′W, E entrance point of Ravine Bay, was charted by the BAE in September 1875 and so named from its shape in plan (BA chart 275, 1877; BPP, 1877, chart facing p. 126; DMR sheet 29ᴬN½, 19ᴬN½ and 9ᴬN½, 1944; CBGN, 1953; DEMR sheet 120 E, 1966; CPCGN, 1980:114).

MUSK-OX BAY 81°44′N 65°17′W, off the N side of Discovery Harbour, Lady Franklin Bay, was charted by the BAE and named *Musk Ox Bay* after the musk ox (*Ovibos moschatus*) frequenting the area (BA chart 275, 1877; BPP, 1877, chart facing p. 62). *Musk-ox Bay* (Greely, 1886, Vol. 1:93; CPCGN Decisions, 1969; CPCGN, 1980:115; DEMR sheet 120 C & 120 D, 1986).

Musk Ox Bay: see Musk-ox Bay.

Musk-ox Valley: see Dodge River.

NAN LAKE 81°13′N 72°20′W, on the S side of the Dodge River, near the NE end of Agassiz Ice Cap, was roughly mapped by the LFBE in May 1883 (Greely, 1886, Vol. 2, map between p. 36 and 37; 1888, Vol. 1:287), and probably named *Lake Nan* at that time (BA chart 275, 1885; DMR sheet 49ᴬs½ and 39ᴬs½, 1944). *Nan Lake* (DEMR sheet 340 D, 1967; CPCGN Decisions, 1968; CPCGN, 1980:116).

Nan, Lake: see Nan Lake.

NARES, CAPE 83°06′N 71°35′W, W entrance point of Markham Fiord, was charted in its outer part by the BAE in May 1876 and named after Captain George Strong (later Vice Admiral Sir George) Nares, RN (1831–1915), in command of the BAE in HMS *Alert*, who had served in HMS *Resolute* (Captain Sir Edward Belcher, RN) on the Franklin search expedition, 1852–54, and in command of the deep-sea expedition in HMS *Challenger,* 1872–74 (BA chart 275, 1877; BPP, 1877, chart facing p. 172, p. 200; GBC, 1910:410; DMR sheet 29ᴬN½, 19ᴬN½ and 9ᴬN½, 1944; DEMR sheet 120 F & 120 G, 1967; CPCGN, 1980:116).

NARES, DÉTROIT DE 80°00′N 70°00′W: see Nares Strait.

NARES STRAIT/NARES, DÉTROIT DE 80°00′N 70°00′W, runs NE-SW from the Lincoln Sea to Baffin Bay, separating Ellesmere Island from North Greenland and comprising Robeson Channel, Hall Basin, Kennedy Channel, Kane Basin, and Smith Sound; was named after Vice Admiral Sir George Nares (*Cape Nares,* q.v.), the second expedition commander, after Captain C.F. Hall, to navigate the entire strait (CPCGN Decisions, 1965; CPCGN, 1980:116; DEMR sheet 120 C & 120 D, 1986; sheet 120 E, 1987).

NARROWS, THE 82°30′N 62°18′W, between Dumbell Bay and Alert Inlet, was charted by the BAE in September 1875 (BPP, 1877, chart facing p. 116; DMR sheet 29ᴬN½, 19ᴬN½ and 9ᴬN½, 1944); named descriptively either by the BAE or later (CBGN, 1953; CPCGN, 1980:116; DEMR sheet 120 E, 1987).

NEBEL, MOUNT 81°02′N 77°57′W, rising to c. 700 m SSE of Cape Gleason, Tanquary Fiord, was roughly mapped by the CLE in May 1915 and named after an American geologist from the University of Illinois (GBC Decisions, 1928; DMR sheet 49ᴬS½ and 39ᴬS½, 1944; CPCGN, 1980:117; DEMR sheet 340 D, 1988).

NEPTUNE REEF 81°34′N 67°00′W, off the mouth of Lonesome Creek, Conybeare Fiord, following the voyage of USCGC *Eastwind* into the fiord in August 1957, was so named after the Roman god of the sea (CBGN, 1960; DEMR sheet 120 C & 120 D, 1967; CPCGN, 1980:118).

NESMITH RIVER 81°50′N 72°44′W, flows SW to Weasel Lake at the E margin of *Henrietta Nesmith Glacier* (q.v.); following field work from the DRB Hazen Camp in 1957−58, was so named in association with the glacier (CBGN, 1960; DEMR sheet 340 D, 1967; CPCGN, 1980:118).

Nesmith River: see Snow Goose River.

NEVILLE, MOUNT 81°11′N 70°33′W, ice-covered and rising to c. 1135 m W of the head of Beatrix Bay, Archer Fiord, was probably sighted by the BAE, but the name *Mount Neville* was applied to a lower peak to the NE of the present feature; the lower peak was climbed on 25 April 1876 (BA chart 275, 1877; BPP, 1877:333 and chart facing p. 336; Greely, 1886, Vol. 1, map p. 390; DMR sheet 29ᴬS½, 19ᴬS½ and 9ᴬS½, 1944). *Mount Neville*, as now applied (CPCGN Decisions, 1969; CPCGN, 1980:118; DEMR sheet 120 C & 120 D, 1986).

NIAGARA GLACIER 81°32′N 75°00′W, flows NE from Viking Ice Cap into the valley of the Lewis River; following field work from the DRB Hazen Camp in 1957−58, was so named from the high waterfalls that flank the glacier in summer (CBGN, 1960; DEMR sheet 340 D, 1967; CPCGN, 1980:118).

NINNIS GLACIER 81°19′N 68°31′W, flowing N towards Archer Fiord from the ice cap on Judge Daly Promontory, was roughly charted by the BAE in April 1876 (BPP, 1877, chart facing p. 336) and named after Staff Surgeon (later Inspector-General) Belgrave Ninnis, MD, RN (d. 1922), of HMS *Discovery* (BA chart 275, 1877; DMR sheet 29ᴬS½, 19ᴬS½ and 9ᴬS½, 1944; DEMR sheet 120 C & 120 D, 1967; CPCGN Decisions, 1969; CPCGN, 1980:119).

North Cooper Key Peak: see Cooper Key, Mount.

NORTH GRANT GLACIER 82°26′N 65°47′W, E of *Mount Grant* (q.v.) flowing NE, was so named in association with the mountain,

following field work by the
Geographical Branch, DMTS, in 1958
(CBGN, 1959; DEMR sheet 120 F &
120 G, 1967; CPCGN, 1980:120).

North Polar Sea: see Arctic Ocean.

NORTH WOOD GLACIER 82°23′N
65°53′W, flowing S from Mount
Grant, was so named in association
with *Mount Wood* (q.v.) to the W
(CBGN, 1959; DEMR sheet 120 F &
120 G, 1967; CPCGN, 1980:121).

NUKAP GLACIER 82°10′N 70°48′W,
W of *Mount Nukap* (q.v.) flowing into
Gilman Glacier, was so named in
association with the mountain (DEMR
sheet 120 F & 120 G, 1967; CPCGN,
1980:121).

NUKAP, MOUNT 82°11′N 70°37′W,
rises to c. 1740 m NE of Gilman
Glacier; following field work from the
DRB Gilman Glacier camp in 1957–58,
was named after the Inughuit traveller
Nukapinguaq, of the Thule District,
North Greenland, who in the 1920s
and 1930s was a member of Danish
expeditions in North Greenland, of
RCMP sledge patrols in Ellesmere
Island, and of the OUELE sledge party
that made the first ascent of Gilman
Glacier (CBGN, 1960; DEMR sheet 120 F
& 120 G, 1967; CPCGN, 1980:121).

OAKLEY RIVER 82°50′N 78°28′W,
flows NE into Maskell Inlet; following
field work by the GSC in 1979, was
named after Gunner Thomas Oakley,
RMA, in HMS *Alert* of the BAE (CPCGN
Decisions, 1980; DEMR sheet 340 E &
340 H, 1988).

OMEGA LAKES 81°27′N 76°27′W, two
lakes N of Redrock Creek and

draining into Rollrock River,
following field work from the DRB
Tanquary Camp in 1962–63, were so
named from their shape in plan
resembling the Greek letter (CPCGN
Decisions, 1965; [shown in error as
one lake] DEMR sheet 340 D, 1967;
CPCGN, 1980:123).

OMINGMAK MOUNTAIN 81°23′N
70°55′W, rises to c. 1090 m NNE of
Hazen Camp; following field work
from the DRB camp in 1957–58, was
named from the Inuit word for musk
ox (*Ovibos moschatus*), which frequent
the area and traces of which were
found on top of the mountain (CBGN,
1960; DEMR sheet 120 C & 120 D,
1967; CPCGN, 1980:123).

OOBLOOYAH CREEK 82°40′N
76°38′W, drains Ooblooyah Glacier
and flows NE into M'Clintock Inlet;
following field work by the GSC in
1965, was named after the Inughuit
dog-driver Ooblooyah, from the Thule
District, North Greenland, a member
of Peary's parties that travelled the
whole N coast of Ellesmere Island in
1906 and that supported the North
Pole journey of 1909 (*Egingwah Bay*,
q.v.) (CPCGN Decisions, 1966; DEMR
sheet 340 E & 340 H, 1967; CPCGN,
1980:123).

OOBLOOYAH GLACIER 82°36′N
77°35′W, flows NE towards
M'Clintock Inlet and is drained by
Ooblooyah Creek (q.v.); following field
work by the GSC in 1965, was so
named in association with the creek
(DEMR sheet 340 E & 340 H, 1967;
CPCGN Decisions, 1971; CPCGN,
1980:123).

OOPIK ISLAND 82°30′N 63°05′W, a very small island in Black Cliffs Bay, was charted by the BAE in May 1876 and so named from the Inuit name for the snowy owl (*Nyctea scandiaca*), whose pellets were found here (BPP, 1877:291; CBGN, 1960; CPCGN, 1980:124; DEMR sheet 120 E, 1988).

OOTAH BAY 82°48′N 76°07′W, on the E side of M'Clintock Inlet, Marvin Peninsula, following field work by the GSC in 1965, was named after the Inughuit dog-driver Ootah (c. 1875–1955), from the Thule District, North Greenland, who was a member of Peary's party that reached the North Pole, 6 April 1909 (CPCGN Decisions, 1966; DEMR sheet 340 E & 340 H, 1967; CPCGN, 1980:124).

Osborn Mountains: see Osborn Range.

OSBORN RANGE 81°25′N 78°25′W, on the NW side of Tanquary Fiord, extending SW-NE from McKinley Bay to Air Force River, and rising to c. 1550 m, was roughly mapped by the CLE in May 1915 and named *Osborn Mountains,* after Henry Fairfield Osborn (1857–1935), American geologist and palaeontologist; Professor of Zoology, Columbia University, 1891–1910, and President, American Museum of Natural History, 1908–33 (Ekblaw *in* MacMillan, 1918:353). *Osborn Range* (GBC Decisions, 1928; DMR sheet 49^As½ and 39^As½, 1944; DEMR sheet 340 D, 1967; CPCGN, 1980:124).

OVIBOS, MOUNT 81°45′N 65°41′W, rising to c. 640 m in twin summits W of *Musk-ox Bay* (q.v.), Discovery Harbour, was charted by the BAE in September 1875 and so named in association with the bay (BA chart 275, 1877; BPP, 1877, chart facing p. 62; DMR sheet 29^As½, 19^As½ and 9^As½, 1944; DEMR sheet 120 C & 120 D, 1967; CPCGN Decisions, 1969; CPCGN, 1980:125).

OXFORD, MOUNT 82°10′N 73°10′W, rising to c. 2210 m NNE of the head of Henrietta Nesmith Glacier, was roughly positioned and first climbed by the OUELE's most northern sledge-party, 1 May 1935, when its height was estimated at 2750 m (*British Empire Range* q.v.); named after Oxford University (Shackleton, 1937:254–56 and end map; CBGN, 1960; Christie, 1962, Map 20; DEMR sheet 340 E & 340 H, 1967; CPCGN, 1980:125). The second ascent of the peak was made by a field party from the DRB Gilman Glacier camp, 22 June 1957, when its height was determined (Hattersley-Smith, 1958:280).

PACKDOG CREEK 81°23′N 66°53′W, on Judge Daly Promontory flowing N to the SE shore of Archer Fiord, was so named following field work by the GSC from the DRB Hazen Camp in 1958, when pack dogs were used (CBGN, 1960; DEMR sheet 120 C & 120 D, 1967; CPCGN, 1980:125).

PARKER BAY 82°48′N 65°20′W, between Hamilton Bluff and Bird Point, Clements Markham Inlet, was charted by the BAE in April 1876 and named after Coxswain James Parker, RN, who accompanied Parry on his journey towards the North Pole from Spitsbergen (Svalbard) in 1827 (BA chart 275, 1877; BPP, 1877, chart facing p. 172; GBC Decisions, 1928; DMR sheet 29^AN½, 19^AN½ and 9^AN½, 1944; DEMR sheet 120 F & 120 G, 1967; CPCGN, 1980:126).

PARR BAY 83°03′N 69°30′W, between Cape Aldrich and Stubbs Point, Arthur Laing Peninsula, was roughly charted by the BAE in April 1876 as between Cape Aldrich and Wood Point, and named after Lieutenant (later Admiral) Alfred Arthur Chase Parr, RN (1849–1914), Second Lieutenant in HMS *Alert*, who supported the northern sledge journey (BA chart 275, 1877; BPP, 1877, chart facing p. 172; GBC, 1910:416; DMR sheet 29ᴬN½, 19ᴬN½ and 9ᴬN½, 1944; [as now defined] DEMR sheet 120 F & 120 G, 1967; CPCGN, 1980:126).

Parry, Cape: see Hecla, Cape.

PARRY, MOUNT 82°06′N 62°50′W, rising to c. 610 m W of Cape Frederick VII, Robeson Channel, was sighted by Kane in June 1854 and named *Mount Edward Parry*, after Rear Admiral Sir (William) Edward Parry (1790–1855), Arctic explorer and Commander of expeditions to the Northwest Passage, 1819–20, 1821–23, and 1824–25, and towards the North Pole from Spitsbergen (Svalbard), 1827; Hydrographer of the Navy, 1925–29 (Acting Hydrographer, 1823–25) (Kane, 1856, Vol. 1, chart facing p. 5); sighted by Hayes in May 1861, and charted by the USNPE in August 1871 and by the BAE in September 1875. *Mount Parry* (Hayes, 1867, chart facing p. 72; BA chart 275, 1875; Ravenstein, 1875, map; BPP, 1877, chart facing p. 38; DMR sheet 29ᴬN½, 19ᴬN½ and 9ᴬN½, 1944; CBGN, 1960; DEMR sheet 120 E, 1966; CPCGN, 1980:126). *Parry Mountain* (Hayes, 1867:374).

Parry Mountain: see Parry, Mount.

PARRY PENINSULA 82°50′N 65°00′W, between Parker Bay and James Ross Bay, terminating in Cape Hecla, was charted by the BAE in April 1876 and named after Rear Admiral Sir Edward Parry (*Mount Parry*, q.v.) (BA chart 275, 1877; BPP, 1877, chart facing p. 172; GBC Decisions, 1910; DMR sheet 29ᴬN½, 19ᴬN½ and 9ᴬN½, 1944; CBGN, 1960; DEMR sheet 120 F & 120 G, 1967; CPCGN, 1980:126).

PATTERSON BAY 82°37′N 63°15′W, between Cape Cresswell and Cape Richardson, was sighted by the USNPE in September 1871 (Davis, 1876:85); named by the USNPE possibly after Robert Wilson Patterson (1850–1910), American journalist with the *Chicago Times*, 1871–73, and with the *Chicago Tribune* from 1873 (Editor-in-Chief, 1899–1910) (BA chart 275, 1875; Ravenstein, 1875, map; BPP, 1877, chart facing p. 126; GBC, 1910:417; DMR sheet 29ᴬN½, 19ᴬN½ and 9ᴬN½, 1944; DEMR sheet 120 E, 1966; CPCGN, 1980:127); charted by the BAE in September 1875 and called *Marco Polo Bay* from the name of a sledge (BPP, 1877, chart facing p. 88).

PATTERSON, MOUNT 82°33′N 64°35′W, rises to c. 1030 m on the W side of the *Patterson River* (q.v.); following field work by the Geographical Branch, DMTS, in 1958, was so named in association with the river (CBGN, 1959; DEMR sheet 120 F & 120 G, 1967; CPCGN, 1980:127).

PATTERSON RIVER 82°36′N 63°25′W, the larger and northern of the two rivers flowing E into *Patterson Bay* (q.v.), following field work by a DRB-GSC party in 1953, was so named in association with the bay (CBGN,

1959; DEMR sheet 120 E, 1966; CPCGN, 1980:127).

PAVY RIVER 81°31'N 64°28'W, flows NE on Judge Daly Promontory into Hall Basin, S of Cape Baird; was roughly mapped by the LFBE in August 1882 and named after Dr. Octave Pavy (d. 1884), expedition surgeon and naturalist, who had been with H.W. Howgate in West Greenland, 1880–81, and who died at Cape Sabine (Greely, 1886, Vol. 1:426; DMR sheet 29ᴬs½, 19ᴬs½ and 9ᴬs½, 1944; CBGN, 1960; DEMR sheet 120 C & 120 D, 1967; CPCGN, 1980:127).

Peculiar Hill: see Rambow Hill.

PER ARDUA GLACIER 81°32'N 76°31'W, flows SW from *Ad Astra Ice Cap* (q.v.) towards Air Force River; following field work from the DRB Tanquary Camp in 1963–64, was so named from the motto of the RCAF, which supported DRB operations in northern Ellesmere Island (CPCGN Decisions, 1965; DEMR sheet 340 D, 1967; CPCGN, 1980:128).

PIPER PASS 82°24'N 68°15'W, runs N-S between the main ice cap of northern Ellesmere Island and Grant Ice Cap to the E; following field work from the DRB Hazen Camp in 1957–58, was so named to mark the flight through the pass in July 1958 of a Piper Supercub floatplane piloted by its owner, Dr. Terris Moore (1908–93), President, University of Alaska, Fairbanks, 1949–53 (CBGN, 1960; Christie, 1962, Map 20; DEMR sheet 120 F & 120 G, 1967; CPCGN, 1980:130).

Polar Sea: see Arctic Ocean.

PORTER BAY 82°42'N 63°40'W, between Cape Delano and the N entrance point of Rowan Bay with its inner part named Dana Bay, was sighted by the USNPE in September 1871 (Davis, 1876:85); named by the USNPE possibly after Admiral David Dixon Porter, USN (1813–91), who served in the Union forces in the American Civil War, 1861–65, and became Superintendent of the U.S. Naval Academy, 1865–69 (BA chart 275, 1875; Ravenstein, 1875, map; BPP, 1877, chart facing p. 126; GBC, 1910:419; DMR sheet 29ᴬN½, 19ᴬN½ and 9ᴬN½, 1944; DEMR sheet 120 E, 1966; CPCGN, 1980:132).

PTARMIGAN CREEK 81°47'N 71°55'W, flows SE into Lake Hazen WSW of Hazen Camp; following field work from the DRB camp in 1957–58, was named after the rock ptarmigan (*Lagopus mutus*), which frequents the area (CBGN, 1960; DEMR sheets 120 C & 120 D, 340 D, 1967; CPCGN, 1980:134).

PULLEN CREEK 82°30'N 62°19'W, flows N from *Mount Pullen* (q.v.) into the W side of Alert Inlet; following field work by the Geographical Branch, DMTS, in 1952, was so named in association with the mountain (CBGN, 1953; DEMR sheet 120 E, 1966; CPCGN, 1980:134).

PULLEN, MOUNT 82°25'N 62°17'W, rising to 580 m near the NE end of Winchester Hills, was charted by the BAE in September 1875 and named after The Reverend Henry William Pullen, RN (1836–1903), Chaplain in HMS *Alert* (BPP, 1877, chart facing p. 172; GBC, 1910:420; DMR sheet 29ᴬN½, 19ᴬN½ and 9ᴬN½, 1944; DEMR sheet 120 E, 1966; CPCGN, 1980:134).

QUARTERDECK PEAK 82°18′N 78°55′W, rises to c. 1890 m between Milne Glacier and Marine Glacier; following its ascent by members of the RNEIE in 1972, was so named descriptively (CPCGN Decisions, 1973; CPCGN, 1980:135; DEMR sheet 340 E & 340 H, 1988).

Rainbow Hill: see Rambow Hill.

RAMBOW HILL 83°02′N 75°08′W, rising to 485 m WSW of Cape Alexandra, was charted by the BAE in May 1876 and named *Ram Bow Hill* from its resemblance to the ram bow of an ironclad battleship (BA chart 275, 1877; BPP, 1877, chart facing p. 172, p. 202); also called *Peculiar Hill* (BPP, 1877, chart facing p. 172). *Rainbow Hill,* in error (DMR sheet 49^AN½, 19^AN½ and 9^AN½, 1944). *Rambow Hill* (CBGN, 1960; DEMR sheet 340 E & 340 H, 1967; CPCGN, 1980:137).

Ram Bow Hill: see Rambow Hill.

RAVINE BAY 82°30′N 62°04′W, between Sickle Point and Mushroom Point, was charted by the BAE in September 1875 and so named from the small ravine at its E side (BPP, 1877, chart facing p. 88; CBGN, 1953; DEMR sheet 120 E, 1966; CPCGN, 1980:138).

RAVINE CREEK 82°29′N 62°00′W, flows N through a ravine into the E side of *Ravine Bay* (q.v.); following field work by the Geographical Branch, DMTS, in 1952, was so named in association with the bay (CBGN, 1953; DEMR sheet 120 E, 1966; CPCGN, 1980:138).

Rawlings Bay: see Rowan Bay.

Rawlinson, Mount c. 82°40′N 68°35′W, rising to c. 1500 m W of the head of Clements Markham Inlet, was roughly charted by the BAE in April 1876 and named after Sir Henry (Creswicke) Rawlinson, 1st Baronet (1810–95), British Assyriologist; President of the Royal Geographical Society, 1871–72 and 1874–75 (BA chart 275, 1877; Nares, 1878, Vol. 1, chart facing p. 1, p. 325; GBC, 1910:425; DMR sheet 29^AN½, 19^AN½ and 9^AN½, 1944). The name was later rescinded through lack of positive identification (CBGN, 1960).

RAWSON, CAPE 82°25′N 61°15′W, rising very steeply to c. 150 m at the SE end of Floeberg Beach, was charted by the BAE in September 1875 and named after Lieutenant Wyatt Rawson, RN (1849–82), Third Lieutenant in HMS *Discovery*, who was killed while serving with naval forces near Khartoum in the first Sudan War (BA chart 275, 1877; BPP, 1877, chart facing p. 116; GBC, 1910:425; DMR sheet 29^AN½, 19^AN½ and 9^AN½, 1944; DEMR sheet 120 E, 1966; CPCGN, 1980:138).

RECORD POINT 81°11′N 69°35′W, between the entrances of Beatrix Bay and Ella Bay, Archer Fiord, was charted by the BAE in April 1876 and so named from the record left there in a cairn (BA chart 275, 1877; BPP, 1877, chart facing p. 336; GBC Decisions, 1910; DMR sheet 29^As½, 19^As½ and 9^As½, 1944; DEMR sheet 120 C & 120 D, 1967; CPCGN, 1980:138).

REDROCK CREEK 81°26′N 76°45′W, flows W into the head of Tanquary Fiord; following field work from the DRB Tanquary Camp in 1962–63, was so named because the creek runs red from the Permian sandstone exposed up its valley (CPCGN Decisions, 1965; DEMR sheet 340 D, 1967; CPCGN, 1980:138).

REDROCK GLACIER 81°27′N 76°11′W, flows SW from Viking Ice Cap and is drained by *Redrock Creek* (q.v.); following field work from the DRB Tanquary Camp in 1962−63, was so named in association with the creek (CPCGN Decisions, 1965; DEMR sheet 340 D, 1967; CPCGN, 1980:138).

REEDS, MOUNT 81°31′N 75°38′W, summit of Viking Ice Cap, rising to c. 1580 m, was sighted by the CLE in May 1915 and named after Chester Reeds, geologist of the American Museum of Natural History (GBC Decisions, 1928; DMR sheet 49^As½ and 39^As½, 1944; CPCGN, 1980:139; DEMR sheet 340 D, 1988).

RICHARDS, CAPE 82°59′N 79°17′W, between Cape Fanshawe Martin and Bromley Island, was charted by the BAE in May 1876 and named after Admiral Sir George (Henry) Richards (1820−1900), in command of HMS *Assistance* on Franklin search expedition, 1852−54; Hydrographer of the Navy, 1864−74 (BA chart 275, 1877; BPP, 1877, chart facing p. 172; GBC, 1910, map; GBC Decisions, 1928; DMR sheet 49^AN½ and 39^AN½, 1944; DEMR sheet 340 E & 340 H, 1967; CPCGN, 1980:140).

RICHARDSON, CAPE 82°34′N 62°55′W, NW entrance point of Black Cliffs Bay, was sighted by the USNPE in September 1871 (Davis, 1876:85); named by the USNPE after Sir John Richardson (1787−1865), who as

Surgeon, RN, and naturalist accompanied Sir John Franklin on his expeditions to the Canadian western Arctic in 1819−22 and 1825−27 (BA chart 275, 1875; Ravenstein, 1875, map; BPP, 1877, chart facing p. 126; GBC, 1910:427; DMR sheet 29^AN½, 19^AN½ and 9^AN½, 1944; DEMR sheet 120 E, 1966; CPCGN, 1980:140); charted by the BAE in September 1875 and called *Depot Point* from a food cache laid there (BPP, 1877, chart facing p. 78).

ROBESON CHANNEL/ROBESON, DÉTROIT DE 82°00′N 61°30′W, runs SW-NE from Hall Basin to the Lincoln Sea and separates NE Ellesmere Island from North Greenland; was sighted by Hayes in May 1861 (Hayes, 1867, chart facing p. 72); charted by the USNPE in September 1871 (Davis, 1876:85); named by the USNPE after George Maxwell Robeson (1829−97), U.S. Secretary of the Navy, 1869−77, and further charted by the BAE in September 1875 and April 1876 (BA chart 275, 1875; Ravenstein, 1875, map; BPP, 1877, chart facing p. 116; GBC, 1910, map; DMR sheet 29^AN½, 19^AN½ and 9^AN½, 1944; sheet 29^As½, 19^As½ and 9^As½, 1944; DEMR sheet 120 E, 1966; sheet 120 C & 120 D, 1967; CPCGN, 1980:141).

ROBESON, DÉTROIT DE 82°00′N 61°30′W: see Robeson Channel.

Roderick Murchison, Cape: see Murchison, Cape.

ROGERS LAKE 81°50′N 68°17′W, W of the head of Black Rock Vale and S of Appleby Lake, was roughly mapped by the LFBE in June 1882 and named

Lake Rogers after L.H. Rogers (Greely, 1886, Vol. 1:373 and map p. 390). *Rogers Lake* (CBGN, 1960; DEMR sheet 120 C & 120 D, 1967; CPCGN, 1980:142).

Rogers, Lake: see Rogers Lake.

ROLLROCK GLACIER 81°32′N 76°03′W, flows NW into the valley of the *Rollrock River* (q.v.) and impounds Rollrock Lake; following field work from the DRB Tanquary Camp in 1963–64, was so named in association with the river (CPCGN Decisions, 1965; DEMR sheet 340 D, 1967; CPCGN, 1980:142).

ROLLROCK LAKE 81°34′N 75°55′W, is impounded by the Rollrock Glacier and drained by the *Rollrock River* (q.v.); following field work from the DRB Tanquary Camp in 1963–64, was so named in association with the river (CPCGN Decisions, 1965; DEMR sheet 340 D, 1967; CPCGN, 1980:142).

ROLLROCK RIVER 81°26′N 76°45′W, drains Rollrock Lake and joins Air Force River to flow SW into the head of Tanquary Fiord; following field work from the DRB Tanquary Camp in 1963–64, was named descriptively, the word "rollrock" being taken from the poem *Inversnaid* (1881) by Gerard Manley Hopkins (CPCGN Decisions, 1965; DEMR sheet 340 D, 1967; CPCGN, 1980:142).

Romain Desfossés, Cape: see Defosse, Cape.

ROUNDEL GLACIER 81°58′N 71°36′W, on the NW side of Glacier Pass and W of the Abbé River, following field work from the DRB Hazen Camp in 1957–58, was named

after the red, white, and blue roundel of the Royal Canadian Air Force, which supported DRB operations (CBGN, 1960; DEMR sheet 120 C & 120 D, 1967; CPCGN, 1980:142).

ROWAN BAY 82°40′N 63°37′W, NW of Cape Cresswell, was sighted by the USNPE in September 1871 (Davis, 1876:85) and so named (BA chart 275, 1875; Ravenstein, 1875, map; BPP, 1877, chart facing p. 126; GBC Decisions, 1910; DMR sheet 29^{A}N½, 19^{A}N½ and 9^{A}N½, 1944; DEMR sheet 120 E, 1966; CPCGN, 1980:143); charted by the BAE in September 1875 and called *Rawlings Bay* after Petty Officer Thomas Rawlings, RN, Captain of Foretop in HMS *Alert* (BPP, 1877, chart facing p. 88).

RUGGLES RIVER 81°42′N 69°18′W, flows SE from Lake Hazen into Chandler Fiord throughout the year, providing the only drainage of the lake; was traversed by the LFBE, 30 April 1882, when the lake was discovered; roughly mapped and named possibly after Brigadier General George David Ruggles (1833–1904), who became Adjutant General, U.S. Army, 1893–97 (BA chart 275, 1885; Greely, 1886, Vol. 1:276 and map p. 390; DMR sheet 29^{A}S½, 19^{A}S½ and 9^{A}S½, 1944; DEMR sheet 120 C & 120 D, 1967; CPCGN, 1980:143).

Saggers Glacier: see Twin Glacier.

SAIL HARBOUR 82°51′N 65°15′W, E of Bird Point, Parker Bay, Clements Markham Inlet, was charted by the BAE in April 1876 and so named because the expedition sledge crews were assisted by sail in crossing the harbour on their outward march (BA chart 275, 1877; BPP, 1877, chart facing p. 172, p. 246; DMR sheet 29^A N½, 19^A N½ and 9^A N½, 1944; DEMR sheet 120 F & 120 G, 1967; CPCGN, 1980:144).

ST. PATRICK BAY 81°47′N 64°09′W, on Robeson Channel between Cape Murchison and Cartmel Point, was charted by the BAE in March 1876 and named *St. Patrick's Bay* in honour of St. Patrick's Day, 17 March (BPP, 1877, chart facing p. 116; Nares, 1878, Vol. 1:120). *St. Patrick Bay* (BA chart 275, 1877; BPP, 1877, chart facing p. 38; GBC Decisions, 1939; DMR sheet 29^A S½, 19^A S½ and 9^A S½, 1944; DEMR sheet 120 C & 120 D, 1967; CPCGN, 1980:144).

St. Patrick's Bay: see St. Patrick Bay.

SALOR CREEK 81°54′N 68°57′W, draining Craig Lake and flowing into the E end of Lake Hazen, was roughly mapped by the LFBE in June 1882 (Greely, 1886, Vol. 1, map p. 390); following field work from the DRB Hazen Camp in 1957–58, named after Corporal Nicholas Salor (d. 1884), of the Second Cavalry, U.S. Army, who had been there on the LFBE (CBGN, 1960; DEMR sheet 120 C & 120 D, 1967; CPCGN, 1980:145).

SCYLLA GLACIER 81°36′N 75°22′W, flows NNE from Viking Ice Cap and, with Charybdis Glacier, impounds Ekblaw Lake and blocks the Lewis River valley; following field work from the DRB Hazen Camp in 1957–58, was so named in association with *Charybdis Glacier* (q.v.) (CBGN, 1960; DEMR sheet 340 D, 1967; CPCGN, 1980:148).

SELF POND 82°27′N 61°59′W, NE of Dean Hill, following field work by the Geographical Branch, DMTS, in 1952, was named after Able Seaman James Self, RN, of HMS *Alert* (CBGN, 1953; DEMR sheet 120 E, 1966; CPCGN, 1980:148).

Seven Sisters: see Seven Sisters Peaks.

SEVEN SISTERS GLACIER 82°05′N 71°10′W, flows NE to join Gilman Glacier on the NW side of *Seven Sisters Peaks* (q.v.); following field work from the DRB Gilman Glacier camp in 1957–58, was so named in association with the peaks (CBGN, 1960; DEMR sheet 120 F & 120 G, 1967; CPCGN, 1980:149).

SEVEN SISTERS PEAKS 82°04′N 71°05′W, run NE-SW to NW of the Gilman River and rise to c. 1700 m; following field work from the DRB Gilman Glacier camp in 1957–58, were so named as consisting of seven main peaks (CBGN, 1960; CPCGN, 1980:149). *Seven Sisters* (DEMR sheet 120 F & 120 G, 1967).

SHERIDAN, CAPE 82°28′N 61°30′W, marking the NW end of *Floeberg Beach* (q.v.), was sighted by the USNPE in September 1871 (Davis, 1876:85); named by the USNPE after General Philip Henry Sheridan (1831–88), Divisional Commander in the Union forces during the American Civil War, 1861–65, and Commanding General, U.S. Army, 1884–88 (BA chart 275, 1875; Ravenstein, 1875, map; BPP, 1877, chart facing p. 126; GBC Decisions, 1910; DMR sheet 29N½, 19^A N½ and 9^A N½, 1944; DEMR sheet 120 E, 1966; CPCGN, 1980:150).

SHERIDAN RIVER 82°28′N 61°28′W, flowing NE into the Lincoln Sea at *Cape Sheridan* (q.v.), was so named by the Peary Expedition, 1908–09, in association with the cape (Borup, 1911:267; CPCGN Decisions, 1962; DEMR sheet 120 E, 1966; CPCGN, 1980:150).

SHERWOOD, MOUNT 81°20′N 75°12′W, rising to c. 1200 m between the Macdonald River and Mount Arthur, was sighted by the CLE in May 1915 and named after George Herbert Sherwood (1876–1937), Director, American Museum of Natural History, 1927–34 (GBC Decisions, 1928; DMR sheet 49ᴬs½ and 39ᴬs½, 1944; CPCGN, 1980:150; DEMR sheet 340 D, 1988).

SICKLE POINT 82°30′N 62°05′W, W entrance point of Ravine Bay, was charted by the BAE in September 1875 and so named from its shape in plan (BPP, 1877:75; CBGN, 1959; DEMR sheet 120 E, 1966; CPCGN, 1980:151); also called *Snow House Point* by the BAE (Nares, 1878, Vol. 1:155).

SILENE CREEK 81°21′N 77°12′W, flows WNW into Tanquary Fiord between Fishhook Point and Tanquary Camp; following field work from the DRB camp in 1967, was named after the moss campion (*Silene acaulis*) found in this area only on the banks of this creek (CPCGN Decisions, 1971; CPCGN, 1980:151; DEMR sheet 340 D, 1988).

Simmond(s) Bay: see Simmons Bay.

SIMMONS BAY 81°15′N 69°20′W, on the NW side of Archer Fiord W of Depot Point, was charted by the BAE in April 1876 and named *Simmonds* [sic] Bay after Petty Officer Thomas

Simmons (or Simmonds), RN, Captain of the Foretop in HMS *Discovery* and a member of the sledge party to Archer Fiord (BPP, 1877, chart facing p. 336; DMR sheet 29ᴬs½, 19ᴬs½ and 9ᴬs½, 1944; DEMR sheet 120 C and 120 D, 1967). *Simmond [sic] Bay,* (BA chart 275, 1877). *Simmons Bay* (GBC, 1910:436; CPCGN, 1980:152; DEMR sheet 120 C & 120 D, 1986).

SIMMONS ICE CAP 81°19′N 68°51′W, NE of *Simmons Bay* (q.v.) and above Archer Fiord, following field work by the PCSP in 1975 was so named in association with the bay (CPCGN Decisions, 1977; CPCGN, 1980:152; DEMR sheet 120 C & 120 D, 1986).

Simmons Island: see Williams Island.

Simmons Point: see Cresswell, Cape.

SKELETON CREEK 81°50′N 71°18′W, flows E into Lake Hazen just N of Hazen Camp; following field work from the DRB camp from 1962, was so named in association with *Skeleton Lake* (q.v.), which it drains (Savile, 1964, map p. 256–57; CPCGN, 1980:152; DEMR sheet 120 C & 120 D, 1986).

SKELETON LAKE 81°50′N 71°29′W, between McGill Mountain and Blister Hill, is drained by Skeleton Creek; following field work from the DRB Hazen Camp from 1962, was so named from a musk-ox skeleton lying on its shore (Savile, 1964, map p. 256–57; CPCGN, 1980:153), but is not shown on DEMR sheet 120 C & 120 D, 1988.

SKELETON VALLEY 81°32′N 69°06′W, N-S pass between the Ida River and the Dodge River, following field work by the PCSP in 1975, was so named from a musk-ox skeleton found there (CPCGN Decisions, 1977; CPCGN, 1980:153; DEMR sheet 120 C & 120 D, 1986).

SMITH PENINSULA 82°30′N 62°52′W, between Black Cliffs Bay and Colan Bay, following field work by the Geographical Branch, DMTS, in 1952, was named after Flight Lieutenant R.S. Smith, DFC, RCAF, who lost his life in World War II (CBGN, 1953; DEMR sheet 120 E, 1966; CPCGN, 1980:154).

SNOW GOOSE RIVER 81°50′N 71°06′W, flows SE into Lake Hazen just ENE of Hazen Camp; following field work from the DRB camp in 1957–58, was so named after the lesser snow goose *(Anser caerulescens)* (CBGN, 1960; DEMR sheet 120 C & 120 D, 1967; CPCGN, 1980:154). *Nesmith River* (q.v.), referring in error to the W arm of this river (DEMR sheet 120 C & 120 D, 1967).

Snow House Point: see Sickle Point.

Sophia Cracroft, Cape: see Cracroft, Cape.

SOUTH GRANT GLACIER 82°26′N 65°38′W, E of *Mount Grant* (q.v.) flowing SE, was so named in association with the mountain following field work by the Geographical Branch, DMTS, in 1958 (CBGN, 1959; DEMR sheet 120 F & 120 G, 1967; CPCGN, 1980:155).

SOUTH WOOD GLACIER 82°21′N 66°14′W, flowing NE towards the head of the Grant River, S of *Mount Wood* (q.v.), was so named in association with the mountain (CBGN, 1959; DEMR sheet 120 F & 120 G, 1967; CPCGN, 1980:156).

STEEPROCK GLACIER 81°31′N 76°09′W, flows NW into the valley of the Rollrock River; following field work from the DRB Tanquary Camp in 1963, was so named from the very steep rock walls of this piedmont glacier, and in association with the nearby *Rollrock Glacier* (q.v.) and *Tumblerock Glacier* (q.v.) (CPCGN Decisions, 1965; DEMR sheet 340 D, 1967; CPCGN, 1980:158).

Stephenson, Cape: see Discovery, Cape.

STONY CAPE 81°37′N 66°07′W, W entrance point of Sun Bay, Lady Franklin Bay, was charted by the BAE in April 1876 and so named descriptively (BA chart 275, 1877; BPP, 1877, chart facing p. 336; DMR sheet 29ᴬS½, 19ᴬS½ and 9ᴬS½, 1944; CBGN, 1960; DEMR sheet 120 C & 120 D, 1967; CPCGN, 1980:159).

STUBBS POINT 83°02′N 69°00′W, SE entrance point of Parr Bay, Arthur Laing Peninsula, was charted by the BAE in April 1876 and called *Point Challenger* after HMS *Challenger* (BPP, 1877:195), but later named *Stubbs Point* after Stoker Thomas Stubbs, RN, of HMS *Alert*, a member of the western sledge party (BA chart 275, 1877; BPP, 1877, chart facing p. 172; GBC, 1910:441; DMR sheet 29ᴬN½, 19ᴬN½ and 9ᴬN½, 1944; DEMR sheet 120 F & 120 G, 1967; CPCGN, 1980:160).

Stuckberry, Cape: see Stuckberry Point.

STUCKBERRY POINT 82°57′N 66°44′W, WNW of Cape Colan, Arthur Laing Peninsula, was roughly charted by the BAE in April 1876 and named *Cape Stuckberry* (BPP, 1877, chart facing p. 172) or *Point Stuckberry* (BPP,

1877:190–91; GBC, 1910:441), after
Petty Officer Thomas Stuckberry, RN,
Captain of the Maintop in HMS *Alert*
and a member of the support party for
the western sledge journey. *Stuckberry
Point* (CBGN, 1960; DEMR sheet 120 F &
120 G, 1967; CPCGN, 1980:160).

Stuckberry, Point: see Stuckberry Point.

SULPHUR CREEK 81°36′N 75°00′W,
flows WSW into the Lewis River;
following field work from the DRB
Hazen Camp in 1957–58, was so
named from the strong smell of
sulphur in the area (CPCGN Decisions,
1968; CPCGN, 1980:160; DEMR sheet
340 D, 1988).

SUN BAY 81°38′N 66°00′W, between
Stony Cape and Cape Clear on the N
side of Lady Franklin Bay, was charted
by the BAE in April 1876 and so named
probably because of its S aspect (BPP,
1877, chart facing p. 336; Greely, 1886,
Vol. 1:93; CBGN, 1960; DEMR sheet
120 C & 120 D, 1967; CPCGN,
1980:160).

SUN CAPE 81°42′N 65°19′W,
W entrance point of Discovery
Harbour, Lady Franklin Bay, was
charted by the BAE and so named
probably in association with *Sun Bay*
(q.v.) (BA chart 275, 1877; BPP, 1877,
chart facing p. 62; DMR sheet 29^{A}S½,
19^{A}S½ and 9^{A}S½, 1944; CBGN, 1960;
DEMR sheet 120 C & 120 D, 1967;
CPCGN, 1980:160).

SUN CAPE PENINSULA 81°38′N
65°40′W, extending NE from *Sun Bay*
(q.v.) to Sun Cape and forming the SW
side of Discovery Harbour, was
charted by the BAE and named *Sun
Peninsula* in association with the bay

(BA chart 275, 1877; BPP, 1877, chart
facing p. 62; Greely, 1886, Vol. 2:72).
Sun Cape Peninsula (DEMR sheet 120 C &
120 D, 1967; CPCGN Decisions, 1969;
CPCGN, 1980:160).

Sun Peninsula: see Sun Cape Peninsula.

SYLVIA MOUNTAIN 81°38′N
66°13′W, rising to c. 630 m above
Stony Cape, Lady Franklin Bay, was
charted by the BAE and so named (BA
chart 275, 1877; BPP, 1877, chart
facing p. 38; DMR sheet 29^{A}S½, 19^{A}S½
and 9^{A}S½, 1944; DEMR sheet 120 C &
120 D, 1967; CPCGN Decisions, 1969;
CPCGN, 1980:162).

TACONITE INLET 82°51′N 78°13′W,
central arm of an unnamed fiord S of
Bromley Peak, following field work
by the GSC in 1965, was so named
from the cherty iron formation
(taconite) exposed in the cliffs (CPCGN
Decisions, 1966; DEMR sheet 340 E &
340 H, 1967; CPCGN, 1980:162).

TACONITE RIVER 82°49′N 78°00′W,
flows NNW into *Taconite Inlet* (q.v.);
following field work by the GSC in
1965, was so named in association
with the inlet (CPCGN Decisions, 1966;
DEMR sheet 340 E & 340 H, 1967;
CPCGN, 1980:162).

TANQUARY CAMP 81°24′N 76°54′W,
following a sealift by CCGS *John A.
Macdonald* (Captain P.M. Fournier) in
August 1962, was established by the
DRB in April 1963 near the SE shore of
the head of *Tanquary Fiord* (q.v.), SW
of the mouth of the Macdonald River
and just N of the mouth of May
Creek; so named in association with
the fiord (CPCGN Decisions, 1965;
DEMR sheet 340 D, 1967; Hattersley-

Smith, 1974:58 and Fig. 32 facing p. 102; CPCGN, 1980:4); maintained by the DRB and manned by summer parties until 1972, then maintained by the PCSP until 1986, when Parks Canada assumed this responsibility, using the camp as field headquarters for park wardens in the Ellesmere Island National Park Reserve. *Tanquary Fiord Camp* (DEMR sheet 340 D, 1988). A runway, constructed on river delta material NE of the camp, is used by light aircraft.

TANQUARY FIORD 81°05′N 79°45′W, extends NE from its entrance between Cape James and Kinley Point, Greely Fiord, to Tanquary Camp and Air Force River at its head; was roughly mapped by the CLE in May 1915, but shown much shortened and distorted; named after Maurice Cole Tanquary (1882–1944), a zoologist on the CLE (Ekblaw *in* MacMillan, 1918:353; GBC Decisions, 1928; DMR sheet 49^As½ and 39^As½, 1944; DEMR sheet 340 D, 1967; CPCGN, 1980:163).

Tanquary Fiord Camp: see Tanquary Camp.

TENT RING CREEK 81°33′N 67°39′W, flows NE into Conybeare Fiord; following field work from the DRB Hazen Camp in 1957–58, was so named from an Inuit tent ring at the mouth of the creek (CBGN, 1960; DEMR sheet 120 C & 120 D, 1967; CPCGN, 1980:164).

THOMPSON, MOUNT 81°15′N 76°57′W, rising to c. 1280 m SE of Fishhook Point, Tanquary Fiord, was sighted by the CLE in May 1915 and named after an American geologist of the University of Illinois (GBC Decisions, 1928; DMR sheet 49^As½ and 39^As½, 1944; CPCGN, 1980:166; DEMR sheet 340 D, 1988).

THORES LAKE 82°39′N 73°41′W, at the head of the *Thores River* (q.v.) W of the terminus of Disraeli Glacier, following field work by the GSC in 1979, was named after Petty Officer John Thores, RN, Ice Quartermaster in HMS *Alert*, a member of sledge parties in support of the BAE northern journey (CPCGN Decisions, 1980; DEMR sheet 340 E & 340 H, 1986).

THORES RIVER 82°36′N 72°41′W, drains *Thores Lake* (q.v.) and flows SE and E into the glacier-covered head of Disraeli Fiord; following field work by the GSC in 1979, was so named in association with the lake (CPCGN Decisions, 1980; DEMR sheet 340 E & 340 H, 1986).

TIMMIA, MOUNT 81°25′N 76°25′W, rises to c. 790 m on the N side of the Macdonald River and E of Tanquary Camp; following field work from the DRB camp in 1967, was named after the moss genus *Timmia*, represented by three species in this area (CPCGN Decisions, 1971; CPCGN, 1980:167; DEMR sheet 340 D, 1988).

TOWNSEND, MOUNT 81°11′N 79°04′W, rising to c. 1150 m NE of McKinley Bay, Tanquary Fiord, was roughly mapped by the CLE in May 1915 and named after Dr. Edgar Jerome Townsend (1864–1955), Professor of Mathematics and Dean of the College of Science, University of Illinois, 1905–13 (GBC Decisions, 1928; DMR sheet 49^As½ and 39^As½, 1944; CPCGN, 1980:168; DEMR sheet 340 D, 1988).

TRAVERSE RIVER 81°41′N 72°02′W, flows N to the SE shore of Lake Hazen, E of Whisler Island; following field work from the DRB Hazen Camp in 1957–58, was so named from a geological traverse made along the river (CPCGN Decisions, 1968; CPCGN, 1980:169; DEMR sheet 340 D, 1988).

TUBORG, LAKE 80°57′N 75°35′W, NE of Antoinette Bay, Greely Fiord, was visited by the LFBE in May 1883 (Greely, 1888:288) and by the CLE in May 1915 (Ekblaw *in* MacMillan, 1918:354–55); roughly mapped by the Danish Thule and Ellesmere Land Expedition in April 1940 and named after the Danish brewing company of Copenhagen, which sponsored the expedition (Vibe, 1948, end map; CPCGN Decisions, 1965; DEMR sheet 340 D, 1967; CPCGN, 1980:170).

TUMBLEROCK GLACIER 81°30′N 76°15′W, flows NW into the valley of the Rollrock River; following field work from the DRB Tanquary Camp in 1963, was so named from the frequent falls of erratic rocks down the terminal ice ramp, and in association with the nearby *Rollrock Glacier* (q.v.) and *Steeprock Glacier* (q.v.) (CPCGN Decisions, 1965; DEMR sheet 340 D, 1967; CPCGN, 1980:170).

TURNABOUT GLACIER 82°09′N 69°09′W, flows SE from the main ice cap of northern Ellesmere Island and is drained by the *Turnabout River* (q.v.); following field work from the DRB Hazen Camp in 1957–58, was so named in association with the river (CBGN, 1960; Christie, 1962, Map 20; DEMR sheet 120 F and 120 G, 1967; CPCGN, 1980:171).

TURNABOUT LAKE 81°58′N 68°34′W, NE of the NE end of Lake Hazen, is drained by the *Turnabout River* (q.v.); following field work from the DRB Hazen Camp in 1957–58, was so named in association with the river (CBGN, 1960; DEMR sheet 120 C & 120 D, 1967; CPCGN, 1980:171).

TURNABOUT RIVER 81°56′N 68°52′W, drains Turnabout Glacier and Turnabout Lake, and flows SE into the NE end of Lake Hazen; following field work from the DRB Hazen Camp in 1957–58, was so named from its extreme deviations of course (CBGN, 1960; DEMR sheet 120 C & 120 D, 1967; CPCGN, 1980:171).

TURNSTONE GLACIER 81°41′N 73°58′W, flows SSE from the main ice cap of northern Ellesmere Island and is drained by the *Turnstone River* (q.v.); following field work from the DRB Hazen Camp in 1957–58, was so named in association with the river (CBGN, 1960; Christie, 1962, Map 20; DEMR sheet 340 D, 1967; CPCGN, 1980:171).

TURNSTONE RIVER 81°40′N 72°50′W, drains Turnstone Glacier and flows NE into the SW end of Lake Hazen; following field work from the DRB Hazen Camp in 1957–58, was named after the ruddy turnstone (*Arenaria interpres*), which frequents the area (CBGN, 1960; Christie, 1962, Map 20; DEMR sheet 340 D, 1967; CPCGN, 1980:171).

TWIN GLACIER 81°16′N 67°58′W, flows N towards Archer Fiord from the ice cap on Judge Daly Promontory in two arms, which join to form the terminal part; was roughly charted by the BAE in April 1876 and called *Saggers Glacier* after Able Seaman John Saggers, RN, of HMS *Discovery* (BPP, 1877, chart facing p. 336); later named descriptively *Twin Glacier* (BA chart 275, 1877; BPP, 1877, chart facing p. 38; DMR sheet 29^{A}s½, 19^{A}s½ and 9^{A}s½, 1944; CPCGN, 1980:172; DEMR sheet 120 C & 120 D, 1988).

UNION, CAPE 82°14′N 61°10′W, between Black Cape and Lincoln Bay, Robeson Channel, was sighted by Hayes in May 1861 and so named "in remembrance of a compact which has given prosperity to a people and founded a nation" [the United States] (Hayes, 1867, chart facing p. 72, p. 374; BA chart 275, 1875; Ravenstein, 1875, map; BPP, 1877, chart facing p. 116; GBC, 1910, map; DMR sheet 29^{A}N½, 19^{A}N½ and 9^{A}N½, 1944; DEMR sheet 120 E, 1966; CPCGN, 1980:173).

UNITED STATES RANGE 82°25′N 68°00′W, extends SSW-NNE from Gilman Glacier to Mount Cheops, rising to c. 1850 m at Mount Eugene and including the Grant Ice Cap; was sighted by Hayes in May 1861, roughly positioned, and named after his schooner *United States* (Hayes, 1867, chart facing p. 72; BA chart 275, 1885; GBC, 1910:447; [extending from 78°00′W to Mount Grant] DMR sheet 29^{A}N½, 19^{A}N½ and 9^{A}N½, 1944; [as now defined] DEMR sheet 120 F & 120 G, 1967; CPCGN, 1980:173).

UPPER DUMBELL LAKE 82°30′N 62°30′W, W of Alert and the eastern of two lakes supplying water to the station, was charted by the BAE in September 1875 and, with *Lower Dumbell Lake* (q.v.), included under the name *Dumb Bell Lakes*, from the disposition of the two lakes in plan (BA chart 275, 1877; BPP, 1877, chart facing p. 126; DMR sheet 29^{A}N½, 19^{A}N½ and 9^{A}N½, 1944); following field work by the Geographical Branch, DMTS, in 1952, named *Upper Dumbell Lake* (CBGN, 1953; DEMR sheet 120 E, 1966; CPCGN, 1980:173).

VANIER, MOUNT 82°05′N 77°45′W, rises to c. 2300 m S of the head of Milne Glacier; following field work from the DRB Tanquary Camp in 1967, was named after Major General George Philias Vanier (1888–1967), Governor General of Canada, 1959–67 (CPCGN Decisions, 1971; CPCGN, 1980:174; DEMR sheet 340 E & 340 H, 1986); first climbed by the RNEIE in July 1972.

VARSITY MOUNTAIN 81°57′N 70°55′W, rising to c. 1400 m NE of Hazen Camp and E of the Abbé River, was so named for the University of Toronto, staff and graduate students of which carried out field work from the DRB camp in 1957–58 (CBGN, 1960; DEMR sheet 120 C & 120 D, 1967; CPCGN, 1980:174).

VERY RIVER 81°38′N 73°03′W, flows NE into the SW end of Lake Hazen and drains, with its tributaries, a wide area SW of the lake; was roughly mapped by the LFBE in July 1882 and named probably after Rear Admiral Samuel Williams Very, USN (1846–1919), who as a magnetician commanded the U.S. Transit of Venus Expedition to Patagonia, 1882–83 (BA chart 275, 1885; Greely, 1886, Vol. 1, map p. 390, p. 393; DMR sheet 49^{A}s½ and 39^{A}s½, 1944; CBGN, 1960; DEMR sheet 340 D, 1967; CPCGN, 1980:174). *Very Valley* (Greely, 1886, Vol. 1:393).

Very Valley: see Very River.

VICTORIA AND ALBERT MOUNTAINS 80°45′N 72°00′W, extending NE to the base of Judge Daly Promontory and rising to c. 1550 m, were sighted by Kane in June 1854 and named after Victoria (1819–1901), Queen of England, 1837–1901, and Albert of Saxe-Coburg-Gotha (1819–61), Prince Consort of England, 1840–61; roughly charted by Hayes in 1861, by the USNPE in 1871, and by the BAE in 1875–76 (Kane, 1856, Vol. 1, chart facing p. 5, p. 300; Hayes, 1867, chart facing p. 72; BA chart 275, 1875; Ravenstein, 1875, map; Nares, 1878, Vol. 1:62; GBC Decisions, 1910; DMR sheet 29ᴬs½, 19ᴬs½ and 9ᴬs½, 1944; DEMR sheet 120 C & 120 D, 1967; CPCGN, 1980:174).

VICTORIA LAKE 82°45′N 63°05′W, W of Cape Richardson, was charted by the BAE in September 1875 and named after the expedition sledge *Victoria* (BA chart 275, 1877; BPP, 1877, chart facing p. 88; DMR sheet 29ᴬN½, 19ᴬN½ and 9ᴬN½, 1944; CBGN, 1960; DEMR sheet 120 E, 1966; CPCGN, 1980:175).

VIEW HILL 82°45′N 63°32′W, rising to c. 275 m N of Cape Delano, Feilden Peninsula, was charted by the BAE in September 1875 and so named descriptively (BPP, 1877, chart facing p. 126; CBGN, 1960; DEMR sheet 120 E, 1966; CPCGN, 1980:175).

View Point: see Delano, Cape.

VIKING ICE CAP 81°30′N 75°40′W, lies within an area bounded clockwise by the valleys of the Lewis, Very,

Macdonald and Rollrock Rivers, and rises to c. 1580 m at Mount Reeds; following field work from the DRB Hazen Camp in 1957–58, was so named from the resemblance of nunataks in the ice cap to the horns of a Viking helmet (CBGN, 1960; DEMR sheet 340 D, 1967; CPCGN, 1980:175). *Viking Ice-cap* (Christie, 1962, Map 20).

Viking Ice-cap: see Viking Ice Cap.

WALKER HILL 83°06′N 74°16′W, highest point on Ward Hunt Island, rising to 415 m, was named after Paul T. Walker (1934–59), American glaciologist with the USAF Ellesmere Island Ice Shelf Project (organized by the AINA in summer 1959), who was evacuated from the island with a fatal illness; U.S. Antarctic Research Program glaciologist at Ellsworth Station, Filchner Ice Shelf, British Antarctic Territory, 1957–58 (CBGN, 1960; DEMR sheet 340 E & 340 H, 1967; CPCGN, 1980:176).

WARD HUNT ICE SHELF 83°08′N 73°45′W, extends from Cape Discovery to Cape Nares and is centred on *Ward Hunt Island* (q.v.); following field work by the DRB-GSC-AFCRC group from a camp on the ice shelf 2 km W of the island in 1954, was so named in association with the island (CBGN, 1960; DEMR sheet 340 E & 340 H, 1967; CPCGN, 1980:176). Massive calving in 1961–62 greatly reduced the extent of the ice shelf (Hattersley-Smith, 1963), but this is not reflected in the DEMR map sheet.

WARD HUNT ISLAND 83°06′N 74°10′W, off the entrance of Disraeli Fiord, is bordered by an ice rise to the N and by the Ward Hunt Ice Shelf elsewhere; was charted by the BAE in May 1876 and named after The Right Honourable George Ward Hunt (1825–77), Chancellor of the Exchequer, 1968, and First Lord of the Admiralty, 1874–77 (BA chart 275, 1877; BPP, 1877, chart facing p. 172; GBC, 1910, map; DMR sheet 49^A^N½ and 39^A^N½, 1944; DEMR sheet 340 E & 340 H, 1967; CPCGN, 1980:176). In 1959, the AFCRC and AINA established a field camp on the N side of the island, which was used by the DRB from 1961 onwards.

WATERCOURSE BAY 81°44′N 64°20′W, between Distant Cape and Cape Murchison, was charted by the BAE and named descriptively (BA chart 275, 1877; BPP, 1877, chart facing p. 62; Nares, 1878, Vol. 2:141–142; CPCGN Decisions, 1967; DEMR sheet 120 C & 120 D, 1967; CPCGN, 1980:177). *Water-course Bay* (Greely, 1886, Vol. 1:82).

Water-course Bay: see Watercourse Bay.

WATERCOURSE CREEK 81°44′N 64°20′W, flowing SSE into *Watercourse Bay* (q.v.), was charted by the BAE and noted for the exposures of readily combustible lignite in its rock walls (BPP, 1877, chart facing p. 62; Nares, 1878, Vol. 2:141–142); named *Water-course Creek* by the LFBE in association with the bay (Greely, 1886, Vol. 1:91). *Watercourse Creek* (CPCGN Decisions, 1967; CPCGN, 1980:177; DEMR sheet 120 C & 120 D, 1986).

Water-course Creek: see Watercourse Creek.

WEASEL LAKE 81°50′N 72°44′W, on the E margin of Henrietta Nesmith Glacier, is fed by the Nesmith River;

following field work from the DRB Hazen Camp in 1957–58, was so named after the weasel (*Mustela erminea*) (CBGN, 1960; CPCGN, 1980:177; DEMR sheet 340 D, 1988).

WHISLER ISLAND 81°40′N 72°20′W, near the SW end and off the SE shore of Lake Hazen, was roughly mapped by the LFBE in July 1882 (Greely, 1886, Vol. 1, map p. 390); following field work from the DRB Hazen Camp in 1957–58, named after Private W. Whisler (*Mount Whisler,* q.v.), a member of the LFBE sledge party in this area (CBGN, 1960; DEMR sheet 340 D, 1967; CPCGN, 1980:178).

WHISLER, MOUNT 82°01′N 74°32′W, rising to c. 2500 m, the second highest peak in northern Ellesmere Island (*Barbeau Peak,* q.v.), was roughly mapped by the LFBE in May 1882 and named after Private William Whisler (d. 1884), of the Seventh Cavalry, U.S. Army, a member of the LFBE sledge party to the area (Greely, 1886, Vol. 1:288 and map p. 390; CPCGN Decisions, 1968; CPCGN, 1980:178; DEMR sheet 340 E & 340 H, 1986); called in error *Mount Whistler* [*sic*] (BA chart 275, 1885); first climbed by a party from the DRB Gilman Glacier camp in June 1961 (Hattersley-Smith, 1970:87–88).

Whistler, Mount: see Whisler, Mount.

WHITE POND 82°27′N 62°52′W, E of Hilgard Bay and S of Kirk Lake, following field work by the Geographical Branch, DMTS, in 1952, was named after Commissioned Engineer George White, RN, of HMS *Alert* of the BAE (CBGN, 1953; CPCGN, 1980:179 DEMR sheet 120 E, 1987).

W.H. Lewis River: see Lewis River.

WILEY, MOUNT 81°39'N 74°10'W,
rises to c. 975 m between Adams
Glacier and Turnstone Glacier;
following field work from the DRB
Hazen Camp in 1957–58, was named
after Flying Officer James Wilson
Wiley, RCAF (1919–43), who was shot
down over France in World War II
(CBGN, 1960; DEMR sheet 340 D, 1967;
CPCGN, 1980:180).

WILLIAMS ISLAND 82°32'N 62°36'W,
in the entrance to Black Cliffs Bay,
was charted by the BAE in September
1875 and called *Simmons Island* after
Leading Seaman John Simmons, RN,
Second Captain of Foretop in HMS
Alert (BPP, 1877, chart facing p. 88);
later named *Williams Island,* probably
from the first name of a number of
sailors and marines in HMS *Alert* (BA
chart 275, 1877; BPP, 1877, chart
facing p. 126; GBC Decisions, 1910;
DMR sheet 29^{A}N½, 19^{A}N½ and 9^{A}N½,
1944; DEMR sheet 120 E, 1966; CPCGN,
1980:180).

WINCHESTER HILLS 82°32'N
62°35'W, run ENE-WSW S of Alert
and rise to 580 m at *Mount Pullen*
(q.v.). The name Winchester,
presumably after the English city, was
originally applied by the BAE to the
low ground on the NNW side of the
hills, but was later applied to the hills.
Winchester Valley (BA chart 275, 1877;
BPP, 1877, chart facing p. 172; DMR
sheet 29^{A}N½, 19^{A}N½ and 9^{A}N½,
1944). *Winchester Hills* (CPCGN
Decisions, 1962; DEMR sheet 120 E,
1966; CPCGN, 1980:181).

Winchester Valley: see Winchester Hills.

WOOD, MOUNT 82°23'N 66°34'W,
rises to c. 1310 m on the SE side of the
United States Range and W of the
headwaters of the *Wood River* (q.v.);
following field work by the
Geographical Branch, DMTS, in 1958,
was so named in association with the
river (CBGN, 1959; DEMR sheet 120 F &
120 G, 1967; CPCGN, 1980:182).

WOOD POINT 83°02'N 69°30'W,
separating the two arms of Parr Bay,
Arthur Laing Peninsula, was charted by
the BAE in April 1876 and named after
Colour Sergeant William Wood, RMLI,
of HMS *Alert,* a member of the western
sledge party (BA chart 275, 1877; BPP
1877, chart facing p. 172; GBC,
1910:453; DMR sheet 29^{A}N½, 19^{A}N½
and 9^{A}N½, 1944; DEMR sheet 120 F &
120 G, 1967; CPCGN, 1980:182).

WOOD RIVER 82°30'N 63°10'W,
flows E into Black Cliffs Bay;
following field work by the
Geographical Branch, DMTS, in 1952,
was named after W. Wood, of HMS
Alert (*Wood Point,* q.v.) (CBGN, 1953;
DEMR sheet 120 E, 1966; CPCGN,
1980:182).

WOOLLEN, CAPE 82°31'N 62°54'W,
W entrance point of Colan Bay, Black
Cliffs Bay, was charted by the BAE in
September 1875 (BPP, 1877, chart
facing p. 126); probably named in
error after Able Seaman William P.
Woolley [*sic*], RN, in HMS *Alert* of the
BAE (CPCGN Decisions, 1963; DEMR
sheet 120 E, 1966; CPCGN, 1980:182).

Wootton, Mount: see Beverley, Mount.

WRANGEL BAY 82°00'N 62°30'W,
marking the NE end of the Black
Cliffs, Robeson Channel, was sighted

by Hayes in May 1861 and named
after Admiral The Baron Ferdinand
Petrovich von Wrangel (1796–1870),
of the Russian Navy, who commanded
the Russian Arctic expedition, 1820–
24, and was the first Governor of the
Russian colonies in Alaska, 1829–35,
and Minister of the Russian Navy,
1855–57; charted by the BAE in
September 1875 and April 1876
(Hayes, 1867, chart facing p. 72, p. 374;
BA chart 275, 1877; BPP, 1877, chart
facing p. 116; GBC Decisions, 1910;
DMR sheet 29ᴬN½, 19ᴬN½ and 9ᴬN½,
1944; DEMR sheet 120 E, 1966; CPCGN,
1980:182).

YELLOWSTONE CREEK 81°23′N
77°01′W, flows NW into Tanquary
Fiord SW of Tanquary Camp;
following field work from the DRB
camp in 1969, was so named in
reference to the creek walls of yellow
Permian sandstone (CPCGN Decisions,
1971; CPCGN, 1980:183; DEMR sheet
340 D, 1988).

YELVERTON LAKE 81°38′N 78°05′W,
in *Yelverton Pass* (q.v.), following field
work from the DRB Tanquary Camp in
1963–64, was so named in association
with the pass (CPCGN Decisions, 1967;
CPCGN, 1980:183; DEMR sheet 340 D,
1988).

YELVERTON PASS 81°40′N 78°20′W,
forms the height of land in the NW-
SE through-valley leading from the
head of Yelverton Inlet to the head of
Tanquary Fiord; following field work
from the DRB Tanquary Camp in
1963–64, was so named in association
with the inlet, which was named by
the BAE in May 1876 after Admiral Sir
Hastings R. Yelverton (1808–78), a
Lord of the Admiralty, 1876–79
(CPCGN Decisions, 1967; CPCGN,
1980:183; DEMR sheet 340 D, 1988).

ZEBRA CLIFFS 82°44′N 76°45′W, SE
of Egingwah Bay, M'Clintock Inlet,
following field work by the GSC in
1965, were so named from the striped
appearance of the rock strata (CPCGN
Decisions, 1966; DEMR sheet 340 E &
340 H, 1967; CPCGN, 1980:183).

References

ARROWSMITH, A. 1794. Map of the World. London. Compiled and published by A. Arrowsmith.

BA (British Admiralty). Chart 275, Arctic sea northward from Baffin Bay. Smith Sound, Kennedy and Robeson Channels, c. 1:900,000, first issue, 21 April 1875, small corrections, April 1876, large corrections, n.d. [1877] [inset: Lady Franklin Sound. Discovery Harbour, 1:150,000], large corrections, August 1885. Great Britain: Hydrographic Department, Admiralty.

BLACKADAR, R.G. 1954. Geological reconnaissance north coast of Ellesmere Island, Arctic Archipelago, Northwest Territories. Geological Survey of Canada Paper 53-10. Ottawa: Department of Mines and Technical Surveys. [Preliminary map 53-10 in pocket: "North coast of Ellesmere Island (east of Markham Bay)," 1:506,880.]

BORUP, G. 1911. A tenderfoot with Peary. New York: Frederick A. Stokes Company.

BPP (British Parliamentary Papers). 1877. Journals and proceedings of the Arctic Expedition, 1875–6, under the command of Captain Sir George S. Nares, R.N., K.C.B. Parliamentary Papers, Vol. 56, No. c-1636. ["Arctic Expedition, 1875–6. Report of proceedings. Between 22nd July, 1875, and 27th October, 1876," by G.S. Nares: 1–38; "Report of general proceedings. From 26th August, 1875, to 30th March, 1876," by H.F. Stephenson: 44–61; "Sledge journal, 3 April to 14 June (1876)," by G. Le C. Egerton: 110–117; "Sledge journal, 3 April to 14 June (1876)," by A.H. Markham: 126–157; "Sledge journal, 3 April to 26 June (1876)," by P. Aldrich: 175–231; "Sledge journal, 8 April to 2 May (1876)," by R.H. Archer: 326–338. Charts: "North Polar Sea," c. 1:10,000,000, facing p. 1; "Davis Strait and Baffin Bay," c. 1:6,000,000, facing p. 38; "Discovery Harbour," c. 1:52,500, facing p. 62; "Track chart of proceedings of H.M. Dog Sledges 'Alert' and 'Challenger' away between Sept. 22nd and Oct. 5th 1875," c. 1:30,000, facing p. 78; "...showing the homeward and outward routes of the sledge parties under the command of Commander Markham, Sept. 25th to Oct. 14th 1875," c. 1:30,000, facing p. 88; "The Bellows Valley," c. 1:30,000, facing p. 96; "Tracks of H.M. Dog-Sledge 'Clements Markham,' between Floeberg Beach and Discovery Harbour," c. 1:240,000, facing p. 116; "Outward and return tracks on the sea ice, extending northward, to 83°20'26"N...," c. 1:400,000, facing p. 126; "Northern shores of Grinnell Land" (north coast of Ellesmere Island from Floeberg Beach to Alert Point), 1:480,000, facing p. 172; "Chart of Archer Fiord," c. 1:240,000, facing p. 336.] Great Britain: House of Commons, Parliament.

BROOKES, R. 1826. The general gazetteer; or compendious geographical dictionary. 18th ed. with additions by A. Picquot. London: C. and J. Rivington, etc. [Map of the Eastern Hemisphere, front.]

CBGN (Canadian Board on Geographical Names). 1948–61. Decisions of the Board. Ottawa: Department of Mines and Resources/Department of Mines and Technical

Surveys. Papers held in the CPCGN Secretariat. Ottawa: Canadian Permanent Committee on Geographical Names, Natural Resources Canada, 615 Booth Street, Rm. 634, Ottawa, Ontario K1A 0E9, Canada.

CENTURY COMPANY. 1897. Century atlas. New York: Century Company. [Map No.3: "North Polar Regions," c. 1:10,000,000.]

CHRISTIE, R.L. 1962. Northeastern Ellesmere Island, District of Franklin. Geological Survey of Canada Paper 61-10. Ottawa: Department of Mines and Technical Surveys. [Preliminary map 20-1962 in pocket: "Geology, northeastern Ellesmere Island, District of Franklin," 1:506,880.]

CPCGN (Canadian Permanent Committee on Geographical Names). 1980. Gazetteer of Canada: Northwest Territories. Ottawa: Department of Energy, Mines and Resources.

———. 1987. Glossary of generic terms in Canada's geographical names. Terminology Bulletin 176. Ottawa: Department of Energy, Mines and Resources.

———. 1990. Principles and procedures for geographical naming. Ottawa: Department of Energy, Mines and Resources.

CPCGN DECISIONS. 1961–94. Decisions of the Committee. Papers held in the CPCGN Secretariat. Ottawa: Canadian Permanent Committee on Geographical Names, Natural Resources Canada, 615 Booth Street, Rm. 634, Ottawa, Ontario K1A 0E9, Canada.

DAVIS, C.H., ed. 1876. Narrative of the North Polar Expedition. U.S. Ship 'Polaris', Captain Charles Francis Hall commanding. Washington, D.C.: Government Printing Office. [Map: "Discoveries of the Polaris," 1:3,200,000, between p. 356–357.]

DEMR (Department of Energy, Mines and Resources). 1:250,000 Map sheets. 120 C & 120 D, Lady Franklin Bay, Edition 1 1967, Edition 2 (rev.) 1986, Edition 3 (interim corrections) 1988; 120 E, Robeson Channel, Edition 1 1966, Edition 2 (rev.) 1987, Edition 3 (interim corrections) 1988; 120 F & 120 G, Clements Markham Inlet, Edition 1 1967, Edition 2 (rev.) 1988, Edition 3 (interim corrections) 1988, Edition 4 (interim corrections) 1993; 340 D, Tanquary Fiord, Edition 1 1967, Edition 2 (rev.) 1988, Edition 3 (interim corrections) 1988; 340 E & 340 H, M'Clintock Inlet, Edition 1 1967, Edition 2 (rev.) 1986, Edition 3 (interim corrections) 1988. Ottawa: Canadian Centre for Mapping.

DICK, L. 1991. The Fort Conger shelters and vernacular adaptation to the High Arctic. SSAC Bulletin 16(1):13–23. Ottawa: Society for the Study of Architecture in Canada.

DMR (Department of Mines and Resources). 1944. 1:506,880 Map sheets. $29^A N\frac{1}{2}$, $19^A N\frac{1}{2}$ and $9^A N\frac{1}{2}$, Markham Inlet; $29^A S\frac{1}{2}$, $19^A S\frac{1}{2}$ and $9^A S\frac{1}{2}$, Kennedy Channel; $49^A N\frac{1}{2}$ and $39^A N\frac{1}{2}$, Challenger Mountains; $49^A S\frac{1}{2}$ and $39^A S\frac{1}{2}$, Greely Fiord. Ottawa: Hydrographic and Map Service, Surveys and Engineering Branch.

DUNBAR, M., and GREENAWAY, K.R. 1957. Arctic Canada from the air. Ottawa: Defence Research Board.

EINPR (Ellesmere Island National Park Reserve). 1991. Management planning program. Newsletter No. 1. Ottawa: Environment Canada, Parks Service.

FORD, W.L., and HATTERSLEY-SMITH, G. 1965. On the oceanography of the Nansen Sound fiord system. Arctic 18(3):158–171.

GBC (Geographic Board of Canada). 1910. Place Names: Northern Canada. Ninth Report, Part IV:229–455. [End map: "(District of) Franklin (NWT)," 1:3,168,000, 1911.] Ottawa: Geographic Board of Canada.

GBC DECISIONS. 1897–1948. Decisions of the Board. Papers held in the CPCGN Secretariat. Ottawa: Canadian Permanent Committee on Geographical Names, Natural Resources Canada, 615 Booth Street, Rm. 634, Ottawa, Ontario K1A 0E9, Canada.

GREELY, A.W. 1886. Three years of Arctic service: An account of the Lady Franklin Bay Expedition of 1881–84 and the attainment of the farthest North. New York, Charles Scribner's Sons. 2 vols. [Maps: "Fort Conger and vicinity," c. 1:160,000, Vol. 1, facing p. 87; "… showing the explorations by Lieut. J.B. Lockwood, U.S. Army, 1882," c. 1,370,000, Vol. 1:305; "Discoveries in Grinnell Land," c. 1:720,000, Vol. 1:390; "Discoveries made in the interior of Grinnell Land…," c. 1:1,200,000, Vol. 2, between p. 36 and 37.]

———. 1888. Report on the proceedings of the United States Expedition to Lady Franklin Bay, Grinnell Land. Vol. 1. Washington, D.C.: Government Printing Office. ["Chart showing excursions of steam launch 'Lady Greely,' during the summer of 1882," c. 1:600,000, between p. 236 and 237. End map: "Grinnell Land, from discoveries made by Inglefield, Kane, Hayes, Hall and Nares," c. 1:1,460,000.]

GREENAWAY, K.R., and COLTHORPE, S.E. 1948. An aerial reconnaissance of Arctic North America. Ottawa: Joint Intelligence Bureau.

HATTERSLEY-SMITH, G. 1956. Northern Ellesmere Island. Geographical Journal 122 (1):13–24

———. 1958. A note on Mount Oxford, northern Ellesmere Island. Geographical Journal 124(2):280–281.

———. 1961a. Northern Ellesmere Island: The Canadian IGY Expedition to Lake Hazen. Beaver, Outfit 292 (Winter):42–47.

———. 1961b. Peary's North Pole journey. Beaver, Outfit 292 (Summer):36–39.

———. 1963. The Ward Hunt Ice Shelf: Recent changes of the ice front. Journal of Glaciology 4(34):415–24. ["Map of Ward Hunt Ice Shelf…," c. 1:1,000,000, Fig. 1, p. 416.]

———. 1964a. Exploration and research in northern Ellesmere Island. Beaver, Outfit 295 (Spring):16–25.

———. 1964b. Fort Conger. Canadian Geographical Journal 49(3):104–115.

———. 1967. Note on ice shelves off the north coast of Ellesmere Island. Arctic Circular (1965–66) 17(1):13–14. Ottawa.

———. 1968. Danish Thule and Ellesmere Land Expedition, 1939–40: Record of 4 May 1940. Arctic Circular (1965–66) 17(2):23–25. Ottawa.

————. 1970. Barbeau Peak. Canadian Geographical Journal 80(3):86–91.

————. 1974. North of latitude eighty: The Defence Research Board in Ellesmere Island. Ottawa: Defence Research Board. [Map in pocket: "Northern Ellesmere Island," 1:1,000,000. Surveys and Mapping Branch, DEMR, 1973.]

————. 1976. The British Arctic Expedition, 1875–76. Polar Record 18 (113):117–126.

————. 1980. The history of place-names in the Falkland Islands Dependencies (South Georgia and the South Sandwich Islands). British Antarctic Survey Scientific Reports No. 101. Cambridge: Natural Environment Research Council, British Antarctic Survey.

————. 1991. The history of place-names in the British Antarctic Territory. British Antarctic Survey Scientific Reports No. 113, Parts 1 and 2. Cambridge: Natural Environment Research, British Antarctic Survey.

HATTERSLEY-SMITH, G., CRARY, A.P., and CHRISTIE, R.L. 1955. Northern Ellesmere Island, 1953 and 1954. Arctic 8(1):3–36.

HAYES, I.I. 1867. The Open Polar Sea. A narrative of a voyage of discovery towards the North Pole in the schooner 'United States.' London: Sampson Low, Son, and Marston. ["Chart of Smith Sound showing Dr. Hayes' track and discoveries. 1860–61," c 1:5,000,000, facing p. 72.]

INGLEFIELD, E.A. 1853. A summer search for Sir John Franklin; with a peep into the polar basin. London: T. Harrison. [End chart: "Arctic Sea. Baffin Bay. Sheet 1," c. 1:2,000,000 (London: Admiralty, 1853).]

KANE, E.K. 1856. Arctic explorations in the years 1853, '54, '55. 2 vols. Philadelphia: Childs and Peterson. ["Chart exhibiting the discoveries of the Second American Grinnell Expedition in search of Sir John Franklin," 1:1,200,000, Vol. 1, facing p. 5.]

KOENIG, L.S., GREENAWAY, K.R., DUNBAR, M., and HATTERSLEY-SMITH, G. 1952. Arctic ice islands. Arctic 5(2):67–103.

MACMILLAN, D.B. 1918. Four years in the white North. London and New York: Harper and Brothers. [Map: "Field work of Crocker Land Expedition...," c. 1:5,300,000, between p. 30–31. Appendix 2:333–370: "On unknown shores: The traverse of Grant and Ellesmere lands," by W.E. Ekblaw.]

NANSEN, F. 1897. Farthest North. 2 vols. New York: Harper and Brothers.

NARES, Sir G.S. 1878. Narrative of a voyage to the Polar Sea during 1875–6 in H.M. Ships 'Alert' and 'Discovery.' London: Sampson Low, Marston, Searle, and Rivington. 2 vols. [Charts: "Smith Sound, Kennedy and Robeson Channels," c. 1:1,000,000, Vol. 1, facing p. 1; "Outward and return tracks on the sea ice, extending northward, to 83°20′26″N...," c. 1:1,000,000, Vol. 2, facing p. 1.]

OLIVER, D.R. 1963. Entomological studies in the Lake Hazen area, Ellesmere Island, including lists of species of Arachnida, Collembola and Insecta. Arctic 16(3):175–180.

PEARY, R.E. 1907. Nearest the pole: A narrative of the polar expedition of the Peary Arctic Club in the s.s. Roosevelt, 1905–06. New York: Doubleday, Page and

Company. [End map: "The polar regions showing the routes and explorations of Robert E. Peary, USN, from 1892 to 1906," c. 1:5,300,000.]

————. 1910. The North Pole. London: Hodder and Stoughton. ["Map of the Arctic regions shewing Commander Peary's route to the North Pole," 1:14,636,160, between p. 316 and 317.]

RAVENSTEIN, E.G. 1875. The Arctic Expedition: Map of the Smith Sound route to the North Polar Sea, [c. 1:3,000,000]. Illustrated London News, 29 May 1875.

SALMON, [Mr.] 1757. The modern gazetteer: Or a short view of the several nations of the world. London: S. and E. Ballard.

SAVILE, D.B.O. 1964. General ecology and vascular plants of the Hazen Camp area. Arctic 17 (4):237–258. ["Sketch map of the Hazen Camp area, showing principal habitats," 1:30,000:256–257.]

SHACKLETON, E.A.A. 1937. Arctic journeys: The story of the Oxford University Ellesmere Land Expedition 1934–5. London: Hodder and Stoughton Limited. [End map: "The Oxford University Ellesmere Land Expedition 1934–5," showing routes followed, c. 1:2,500,000.]

STAFFORD, M.P. 1954. The Peary flag comes to rest. National Geographic Magazine 106:519–532.

SVERDRUP, O. 1904. New land: Four years in the Arctic regions. 2 vols. London: Longmans, Green, and Co. ["Map showing the field work of the Second Norwegian Polar Expedition in the 'Fram'...1898–1902," 1:2,000,000, Vol. 2, in pocket.]

TIMES. 1899. The 'Times' Atlas. London: Office of the 'Times.' [Maps 11–12: "North Polar Regions," 1:20,000,000.]

VIBE, C. 1948. Langthen og nordpaa: Skildringer fra "Den Danske Thule–og Ellesmereland–Ekspedition 1939–40." Copenhagen: Gyldendal. [End map (untitled) to show expedition journeys, c. 1:14,000,000.]

Appendix I:
Geographical Names by Expedition or Agency

Listed below are the 382 geographical names that had been adopted by the CPCGN for official use in the Ellesmere Island National Park Reserve and adjoining areas by the end of 1994. The first 366 names are listed chronologically by the expedition or agency that originally applied the names, or that recommended the application of the names or the need to name certain features. A further 16 names, listed at the end, appear to have been applied by the names authority without recommendation from outside. It should be noted that the names currently adopted by no means always agree with the original applications or recommendations, often differing in generic parts and occasionally in specific parts.

Edward Augustus Inglefield, 1852
Ellesmere Island (Ellesmere, Île d')

Elisha Kent Kane, 1853−55
Beaufort, Mount
Beechey, Cape
Bellot Island
Cracroft, Cape
Defosse, Cape
Grinnell, Mount
Kennedy Channel
Lady Franklin Bay
Murchison, Cape
Parry, Mount
Victoria and Albert Mountains

Isaac Israel Hayes, 1860−61
Church Peak
Frederick VII, Cape
Lieber, Cape
Union, Cape
United States Range
Wrangel Bay

Charles Francis Hall,
Sidney O. Budington, 1871−73
Baird, Cape
Belknap, Cape

Black Cape
Cresswell, Cape
Delano, Cape
Hall Basin
Hamilton Fish Peak
Hilgard Bay
Joseph Henry, Cape
Julia, Mount
Lincoln Bay
Lincoln Sea (Lincoln, Mer de)
Mary Peak
Patterson Bay
Porter Bay
Richardson, Cape
Robeson Channel (Robeson, Détroit de)
Rowan Bay
Sheridan, Cape

George Strong Nares, 1875−76
Albert Edward, Cape
Aldrich, Cape
Alexandra, Cape
Alexandra Lake
Archer Fiord
Ayles Fiord
Ayles Point
Beatrix Bay

Bellows Valley, The
Bethel Peak
Beverley, Mount
Bird Point
Black Cliffs
Black Cliffs Bay
Black Rock Vale
Breakwater Island
Breakwater Point
Bromley Peak
Bulleys Lump
Campbell, Mount
Cartmel Point
Challenger Mountains
Cheops, Mount
Clear, Cape
Clements Markham Inlet
Colan, Cape
Columbia, Cape
Conybeare Fiord
Cooper Key, Mount
Crozier Island
Dana Bay
Dean Hill
Depot Point
Discovery, Cape
Discovery Harbour
Disraeli Fiord
Disraeli, Mount
Distant Cape
Doidge Bay
Dumbell Bay
Ella Bay
Feilden Peninsula
Floeberg Beach
Foster, Mount
Gable Cliff
Gap Mountain
Giffard Peak
Gladstone, Mount
Good Point
Grant, Mount
Guide Hill

Hamilton Bluff
Hare Point
Hecla, Cape
Hogback Mountain
Hornby, Mount
James Ross Bay
Jolliffe Bay
Judge Daly Promontory
Keppel Head
Knot Bay
Lower Dumbell Lake
M'Clintock Inlet
Markham Fiord
Miller Island
Moss, Point
Murray Island
Mushroom Point
Musk-ox Bay
Nares, Cape
Narrows, The
Neville, Mount
Ninnis Glacier
Oopik Island
Ovibos, Mount
Parker Bay
Parr Bay
Parry Peninsula
Pullen, Mount
Rambow Hill
Ravine Bay
Rawson, Cape
Record Point
Richards, Cape
Sail Harbour
St. Patrick Bay
Sickle Point
Simmons Bay
Stony Cape
Stubbs Point
Stuckberry Point
Sun Bay
Sun, Cape
Sun Cape Peninsula

Sylvia Mountain
Twin Glacier
Upper Dumbell Lake
Victoria Lake
View Hill
Ward Hunt Island
Watercourse Bay
Williams Island
Winchester Hills
Wood Point

Adolphus Washington Greely, 1881–84
Abbé Glacier
Adams River
Agassiz Ice Cap
Appleby Lake
Arthur, Mount
Biederbick Lake
Biederbick, Mount
Carolyn Lake
Chandler Fiord
Clay Island
Cobb River
Conger Range
Connell, Mount
Craig Lake
C.S. Smith, Mount
Dodge River
Dyas Island
Eugene, Mount
Fort Conger
Garfield Range
Gatter Island
Gilman Glacier
Hazen, Lake
Heintzelman Lake
Henrietta Nesmith Glacier
Ida Bay
Johns Island
Kilbourne Lake
Lewis River
Lynn, Mount

Nan Lake
Pavy River
Rogers Lake
Ruggles River
Very River
Watercourse Creek
Whisler, Mount

Robert Edwin Peary, 1898–1902, 1905–06, 1908–09
Sheridan River

Donald Baxter MacMillan, 1913–17
Bent Glacier
Bowman, Mount
Burke Bay
Chapman Glacier
Cleaves Glacier
Fernald, Cape
Fiala Glacier
Gleason, Cape
Kennedy, Mount
Koch, Mount
McKinley Bay
Macoun, Cape
Nebel, Mount
Osborn Range
Reeds, Mount
Sherwood, Mount
Tanquary Fiord
Thompson, Mount
Townsend, Mount

Gordon Noel Humphreys, 1934–35
British Empire Range
Oxford, Mount

James van Hauen, 1939–40
Tuborg, Lake

Canadian Meteorological Service, 1950
Alert

Canadian Geographical Branch, 1952, 1958
Alert Creek
Alert Inlet
Bowery Inlet
Cache Creek
Cairn Butte
Colan Bay
Egerton Creek
Egerton Lake
Grant River
Hilgard Lake
Hilgard, Mount
Hilgard River
Hollins Creek
Joiner Creek
Jolliffe, Cape
Kirk Creek
Kirk Lake
Mann Bay
Mann River
May Creek
Moss Pond
North Grant Glacier
Patterson, Mount
Pullen Creek
Ravine Creek
Self Pond
Smith Peninsula
South Grant Glacier
White Pond
Wood, Mount
Wood River

Canadian Defence Research Board (and associated agencies), 1953–72

From Alert, 1953
Eugene Glacier
James Ross River
Moss Bay
Patterson River

From Ward Hut Ice Shelf Camp, 1954
Borup Point
Bromley Island
Disraeli Creek
Marvin Islands
Ward Hunt Ice Shelf

From Hazen Camp, 1957–68
Abbé River
Adams Glacier
Arrow Glacier
Atka Lake
Blister Creek
Blister Hill
Blister Ice Cap
Boulder Hills
Bridge Glacier
Charybdis Glacier
Clements Markham Glacier
Clements Markham River
Cuesta Creek
Divide Glacier
Dryas Glacier
Eastwind Bay
Ekblaw Lake
Glacier Pass
Hazen Camp
Henrietta River
Ida River
Kensington Lake
Kensington River
Lewis Lake
Lonesome Creek

McGill Mountain
Mesa Creek
Neptune Reef
Nesmith River
Niagara Glacier
Omingmak Mountain
Packdog Creek
Piper Pass
Ptarmigan Creek
Roundel Glacier
Salor Creek
Scylla Glacier
Skeleton Creek
Skeleton Lake
Snow Goose River
Sulphur Creek
Tent Ring Creek
Traverse River
Turnabout Glacier
Turnabout Lake
Turnabout River
Turnstone Glacier
Turnstone River
Varsity Mountain
Viking Ice Cap
Weasel Lake
Whisler Island
Wiley, Mount

From Gilman Glacier Camp, 1957–61, 1967
Air Force Glacier
Arrowhead Mountain
Barbeau Peak
Barrier Glacier
Barrier Lake
Commonwealth Mountain
Crescent Glacier
Disraeli Glacier
Fork Mountain
Gilman River
Gypsum River
M'Clintock Glacier

Nukap, Mount
Seven Sisters Glacier
Seven Sisters Peaks

From Tanquary Camp, 1963–72
Ad Astra Ice Cap
Air Force River
Fishhook Point
Green Valley
Gull Glacier
Kettle Lake
Macdonald River
May Creek
Omega Lakes
Per Ardua Glacier
Redrock Creek
Redrock Glacier
Rollrock Glacier
Rollrock Lake
Rollrock River
Silene Creek
Steeprock Glacier
Tanquary Camp
Timmia, Mount
Tumblerock Glacier
Vanier, Mount
Yellowstone Creek
Yelverton Lake
Yelverton Pass

Arctic Institute of North America, 1959–60
Walker Hill

Canadian Department of National Defence, 1962
Alert, Canadian Forces Station (Alert, Station des Forces Canadiennes)

Geological Survey of Canada, 1965, 1979, 1980
Ayles, Mount
Cranstone Peninsula

Crash Point
Egingwah Bay
Egingwah Creek
Ferbrache Peninsula
Harley Ridge
Lorimer Ridge
Marvin Peninsula
Maskell Inlet
Murphy Point
Oakley River
Ooblooyah Creek
Ooblooyah Glacier
Ootah Bay
Taconite Inlet
Taconite River
Thores Lake
Thores River
Zebra Cliffs

**Canadian Polar Continental Shelf
Project, 1972, 1975, 1977**
Christiansen Lake
Jaeger Creek
Murray Ice Cap
Simmons Ice Cap
Skeleton Valley

**Royal Naval Ellesmere Island
Expedition, 1972**
Capstan Peak
Commando Peak
Marine Glacier
Quarterdeck Peak

**Canadian Department of Indian
Affairs and Northern
Development, 1975**
Arthur Laing Peninsula

**Geographic Board of Canada,
1897–1948**
Arctic Ocean (Arctique, Océan)
Murray Lake

**Canadian Board on Geographical
Names, 1948–61**
Daly River
Giffard Bay
Grant Ice Cap
North Wood Glacier
South Wood Glacier

**Canadian Permanent Committee on
Geographical Names, 1961–94**
de Vries Glacier
Dumbell Creek
Ellesmere Island National Park
   Reserve (Île-d'Ellesmere, Réserve
   de Parc National de l')
Hilgard Creek
Mann Point
Milne Glacier
Nares Strait (Nares, Détroit de)
Nukap Glacier
Woollen, Cape

Appendix II: Historic Sites

Historic (as opposed to prehistoric) sites within the present map area are listed below in chronological order of the expeditions involved. The list cannot be regarded as exhaustive.

British Arctic Expedition, 1875–76

From HMS *Alert*

1. A cairn on the summit of Crozier Island was built by Lieutenant P. Aldrich on 18 April 1876 on the outward leg of his western sledge journey. The record it contained was recovered by a DRB-GSC field party from Alert on 5 June 1953 (reproduced in Hattersley-Smith et al., 1955:33).
2. The grave of Niels Christian Petersen, the Danish interpreter on the expedition, lies a short distance above Floeberg Beach. He died on 14 April and was buried on 19 April 1876. The grave consists of a rectangular slab of local rock, with an oak headboard and inscription on a copper plaque.
3. A pile of rocks near sea level at Cape Colan marks the site of a food cache laid by Lieutenant G.A. Giffard on 22 April 1876 in support of the western sledge journey.
4. A cairn (now collapsed) on the highest point of Hamilton Bluff was built on 14 May 1876 by Lieutenant Giffard, while in support of the northern and western sledge parties. The record it contained was recovered by a DRB field party from Lincoln Bay in August 1972 (reproduced in facsimile in Hattersley-Smith, 1974, photo facing p. 38).
5. On a hill about 15 km south of Floeberg Beach, a field camp was made by Lieutenant Giffard and Sub-Lieutenant C.J.M. Conybeare on 5 July 1876. Items of equipment, including clothing and a sleeping bag, were recovered from the site by a DRB-GSC field party from Alert in August 1953 (Hattersley-Smith, 1956:18 and photo facing p. 21).
6. On the hill above Floeberg Beach stands the massive *Alert* cairn, probably constructed in July 1876 shortly before the ship's departure southwards and containing a record left by Captain G.S. Nares. It was visited on 11 April 1882 by Dr. O. Pavy, of the LFBE, who left his own record but did not remove the Nares record. On 5 September 1905, from his ship *Roosevelt* anchored nearby, Commander R.E. Peary recovered the Nares record; he made no mention of finding Pavy's record.

From HMS *Discovery*

1. Ashore at Discovery Harbour late in 1875, Captain H.W. Stephenson built a magnetic observatory and a pendulum hut, the sites of which can still be seen. A large "post office" cairn, originally surmounted by a ship's spar, still stands

near the beach, with a heap of rusted cans of tinned food nearby (Hattersley-Smith, 1964b:105).

2. On the summit of Mount Campbell, Bellot Island, the expedition built a cairn containing a record, which was recovered by a PCSP field party in the 1972 summer.

3. At Record Point, near the head of Archer Fiord, Lieutenant R.H. Archer built a small cairn containing a record, which was also recovered by the PCSP in 1972.

Lady Franklin Bay Expedition, 1881–84

1. Ashore at Discovery Harbour late in 1881, Lieutenant A.W. Greely built a large living hut and a small workshop hut, of which only the foundations can now be seen. He named the station Fort Conger (Hattersley-Smith, 1964b; Dick, 1991).

2. On 4 May 1882, during his journey westward to Lake Hazen and beyond, Greely built a cairn near the terminus of Henrietta Nesmith Glacier. The record it contained was recovered by a DRB field party from Hazen Camp in May 1957, but was too badly damaged by moisture for legibility (Hattersley-Smith, 1961a:43).

Peary Arctic Expedition, 1898–1902

1. Peary with a small party spent part of the winter of 1898–99 at Fort Conger, where he dismantled Greely's large hut to build three small huts, standing now in severe disrepair (Hattersley-Smith, 1964b).

Peary Arctic Expedition, 1905–06

1. At the east end of Lake Hazen, a stone house was found by a DRB field party from Hazen Camp in 1958 (Hattersley Smith, 1961a:43). It had been used by Peary's Inughuit hunters in the 1905–06 winter.

2. During his journey westward along the north coast of Ellesmere Island in 1906, Peary built a large cairn on the peak just east of Mount Cooper Key, near Cape Columbia. The cairn contained a piece of his United States flag and a record dated 8 June 1906 (reproduced in facsimile in Stafford, 1954:525). These were recovered by a DRB-GSC field party from *Alert* on 13 May 1953 (Hattersley-Smith, 1956:17).

3. A short distance north of the *Alert* cairn near Floeberg Beach, Peary built a large cairn surmounted by a cross of sledge runners, facing north and inscribed in the centre with the letter "R" for his ship *Roosevelt*. In the *Alert* cairn Peary deposited his own record, which was recovered on 4 August 1948 by Captain George J. Dufek, USN, commanding United States Task Force 80 in USS *Eastwind*.

4. In a cairn near Floeberg Beach, the engineers G.A. Wardwell and M.J. Maloney left a record in a cairn dated 26 June 1906. The record was recovered by United States Task Force 80 on 5 August 1948.

Peary Arctic Expedition, 1908–09

1. In December 1908, D.B. MacMillan built a cairn at Cape Aldrich to mark his tide-gauge station. The record he deposited was recovered by the Third Thule Expedition, but was irreparably damaged by the expedition's dogs (see below).

2. In March 1909, in support of Peary's return journey from the North Pole, MacMillan left a sledge and cache of fuel, marked by a small cairn, near the north shore of Ward Hunt Island. His record from the cairn was recovered by a DRB-GSC-AFCRC field party in July 1954 (reproduced in facsimile in Hattersley-Smith, 1961b:36).

3. At Cape Aldrich, in June 1909, members of the expedition erected a signpost with four arms commemorating the principal points reached by their Commander on his exploratory journeys (Peary, 1910, photo facing p. 312; Borup, 1911:273).

4. Near Floeberg Beach, Peary erected a cross in memory of Ross G. Marvin, who was drowned on 10 April 1909, while returning to Cape Columbia in charge of a support party for the North Pole journey (Peary, 1910, photo facing p. 302).

Third Thule Expedition, 1919–20

1. In March 1920, Captain Godfred Hansen, Royal Danish Navy, left a cache of food and fuel at Cape Columbia for Captain Roald Amundsen, in support of his aborted drift across the Arctic Ocean in the *Maud*, 1918–20. The cache also included a triple-barrelled shotgun-rifle with ammunition, and despatches and mail for Amundsen. The shotgun-rifle and documents were recovered by a DRB-GSC field party from *Alert* on 12 April 1953 (Hattersley-Smith, 1956:17, 1964a:22).

2. In MacMillan's cairn nearby, Hansen left a record recovered at the same time as the above (reproduced in Hattersley-Smith et al., 1955:34).

Danish Thule and Ellesmere Land Expedition, 1939–40

During their journey back from the west coast of Ellesmere Island in April 1940, the northern sledge party under J. van Hauen left a food cache under a cairn near the bottom of a deep ravine leading northeastward from Lake Tuborg. Van Hauen's record was recovered from the cairn by a DRB field party from Tanquary Camp in July 1967 (reproduced in facsimile in Hattersley-Smith, 1968:24).